MANAGING
THE FUTURE

ALSO BY ROBERT B. TUCKER

Winning the Innovation Game
(with Denis Waitley)

MANAGING THE FUTURE

10 Driving Forces of Change for the '90s

Robert B. Tucker

G. P. PUTNAM'S SONS
New York

G. P. Putnam's Sons
Publishers Since 1838
200 Madison Avenue
New York, NY 10016

Copyright © 1991 by Robert B. Tucker
All rights reserved. This book, or parts thereof,
may not be reproduced in any form without permission.
Published simultaneously in Canada

Library of Congress Cataloging-in-Publication Data

Tucker, Robert B., date.
    Managing the future: 10 driving forces of change for the '90s
Robert B. Tucker.
        p.   cm.
    Includes index.
    1. Success in business. 2. Management. 3. Competition.
I. Title.
HF5386.T828   1991   90-44903 CIP
658.4—dc20
ISBN 0-399-13576-6

Printed in the United States of America
1 2 3 4 5 6 7 8 9 10
This book is printed on acid-free paper.
∞

ACKNOWLEDGMENTS

I would like to extend my thanks and sincere appreciation to a number of people who helped make this book possible.

—To my wife, Carolyn, whose love, support and sense of humor make life an adventure.

—To my daughter, Cara Rose, who came to us during the writing of this book and in whose face I glimpse the future.

—To Jesse Berst, author, colleague and friend. Thank you for being the "driving force" in helping me bring the ideas in this book to fruition.

—To the executives who accepted my invitation to read the work-in-progress and attend a "focus group" at the Los Angeles airport Sheraton in March 1990. Thanks to Anthony Kane, Mary Jane Wagle, Roger Selbert, Mark Frandsen, Robin Brown, George Schmutz, Leland Russell, Ray Broderick, Reg Wilson and Gene Mahn.

—To Helen Peters, whose brainstorming sessions during her visits to Santa Barbara always produce new possibilities.

—To my colleagues who read and strengthened the manuscript: Edwin Rigsbee, Ralph Tucker, Michael LeBoeuf, Neil Baum, and to John Parikhal, for his generous assistance with the jacket copy.

—To my research team: J. Patrick O'Hara, John Boal and Steven Brooks.

—To my innovative literary agent, Jeff Herman, and to my new friends at G. P. Putnam's Sons for their dedication and vision.

To my wife, Carolyn

CONTENTS

INTRODUCTION: HOW TO PROFIT FROM CHANGE

Two years after *In Search of Excellence* reported on forty-three of the "best run" companies in America, fourteen of the forty-three firms were in financial trouble. The reason, according to a *Business Week* study: "failure to react and respond to change."

Today, increasing numbers of businesses are devastated by changes they failed to notice, failed to truly understand and failed to creatively respond to. Avon and Tupperware failed to recognize that women were entering the work force in record numbers and that their distribution systems would have to change to keep pace. Polaroid invested heavily in Polavision while Japanese manufacturers introduced the camcorder and videocassette recorder, which allowed for instant playback. Western Union continued to hold on to the telegram as its mainstay, long after telegrams were becoming obsolete. Dairy Queen continued to see itself as a milk shake stand while other fast food concerns moved forward with greater choices, more modern facilities and more consistent quality.

As I travel the corporate speaking circuit, consulting and meeting with business leaders in a wide variety of industries, I hear a common refrain: The pace of change has exploded. In industry after industry I learn of companies that have been severely crippled or destroyed because of an inadequate or inappropriate response to rapid change: the Beverly Hills real estate syndicator that did not respond to changes in the tax laws; the office products dealers in Boston forced to close because of competition from a new office supplies superstore; the Minneapolis resort that nearly had to cancel its summer season for lack of employees.

These businesses large and small all have something in common: They were blindsided by one or more predictable, structural changes that are now transforming the U.S. economy. And here's the sad part: If those companies had been prepared, these forces could have been their salvation instead of their doom.

Businesses that do not know how to change with change, that do not adapt and respond, do not survive. They become takeover targets, or are merged, purged and submerged out of existence. They go bankrupt; they disappear into oblivion. The reality is, being devastated by change can happen to any business that isn't taking specific steps to positively affect its future by the attitudes and actions it exhibits today.

And that's what this book is about. It shows you how to make change a competitive advantage instead of a drawback; how to prosper instead of merely survive; how to get and keep the mind-set that turns you from a victim into a victor. When you've finished this book, you'll understand why and how change can rocket you into the future and put you far ahead of the competition. You'll have learned from dozens of case histories, both blazing successes and bitter failures. And you'll have specific, hands-on techniques you can use to get started today.

This chapter is an important first step. It introduces the cornerstone concepts of this book. In later chapters, I'll show you how to turn these concepts into weapons, how to arm yourself with an arsenal of ideas. Before you can fight back, though, you must realize that you're in a war. You must understand that the greatest challenge you face in the next decade is the oncoming, overwhelming, accelerating pace of change.

THE ENORMOUS CHALLENGE OF CHANGE

You've got a problem. No, it's not whether to switch to an overseas supplier for your components, or how to get a better discount from your distributor or how to cut the costs of health care benefits. It's a much bigger problem. One that threatens to crush your company.

It's change. Examples of what can go wrong are as near as this morning's newspaper. Customers suddenly desert your product for one that incorporates new technology. A labor shortage renders you unable to fill frontline positions. A lifestyle change makes your services obsolete and unwanted.

Change comes so rapidly today, from so many sides, that it may seem like a random bombardment. In reality, the important developments are manifestations of the ten Driving Forces of change—deep-seated shifts that will dramatically impact *every* business in the 1990s. Once you understand what these forces are and how they work, you are well on the way to getting them on your side.

The Challenge of the Driving Forces

What are the forces of change I referred to above? Here are the names I've given them:

1. Speed
2. Convenience
3. Age Waves

11

4. Choice
5. Lifestyle
6. Discounting
7. Value-Adding
8. Customer Service
9. Techno-Edge
10. Quality

We'll explore each Driving Force in the chapters ahead. You'll see how these forces act in different ways to affect your business and your customers, and you'll gain powerful new ideas you can use to take advantage of each one. But first let's be clear on the meaning of this important concept: A Driving Force is a fundamental value that influences consumer behavior. Unlike a fad or even a trend, both of which are of a more finite and limited duration, a Driving Force is a longer-lasting and profound societal direction.

Now here's the key point of this book: *Within each Driving Force are both threats and opportunities.* To survive and prosper in the nineties, a business must constantly seek competitive advantages from these imperatives. It must find a superior response to each one, and it must do so ahead of the competition.

How prepared are you and your company to withstand the ten Driving Forces? More than that, can you profit from them? I believe you can, provided you change your outlook in two fundamental arenas of business strategy.

HOW TO MEET THE CHALLENGE OF CHANGE

If you want to do more than understand the Driving Forces, if you want to *exploit them for competitive advantage,* then you need two crucial skills. You must know:

- how to manage the future instead of the past
- how to be an attacker instead of a defender

Let's take these one at a time.

Managing the Future vs. Managing the Past

What does it mean to "manage the future"? It means riding the forces of change in the direction in which they're already headed. It means paying attention to change of all types—social, cultural, economic, demographic, regulatory, lifestyle, technological and global—and trying to see patterns in that change.

That's the passive part, or at least the thinking part. Managing the future also has an implication of action—actions designed to create and shape the future. Thus, managing the future also means responding to change through constant innovation, constant improvement. Innovation is coming up with ideas and bringing them to life. But not just any ideas, only those that serve the needs of a customer group. Future-managing companies exploit the changes in their customers' lives, in their markets and in the larger society, rather than simply reacting to them or waiting to see what others do.

Yet another part of managing the future is not nearly as incremental. It involves sussing out and meeting new and emerging customer needs and wants, and creating new opportunities for customers in the way of products and services. But before we talk further about managing the future, we need to look at the dangers of managing the past.

How to Manage the Past

Companies that are managing the past are often the last to know it. And certainly, the last to admit it. Even if they admit it, they will tell you it doesn't matter. Some of them get away with it for years. Their customers may hate dealing with them, but those customers don't feel they have a choice. It's like the only gas station on the mountain. You may not like the prices, or the rude attendant, but you fill up your tank anyway, cursing under your breath.

But businesses that manage the past are living on borrowed time. The reason comes down to one word: customers. Forget about everything else, it's what customers do that counts. If the customer is loyal, all else is secondary. And that's the point: There is a difference between a customer and a *loyal* customer. The American education system, whatever its other faults, still does an excellent job of teaching consumers to vote with their feet. Businesses that manage the past have a tenuous relationship with their customers.

Businesses that manage the future *build* loyal customers. Constantly. When customers change, they change. They strive to be slightly ahead of their customers, as opposed to slightly behind. It's not as if they have a lock on customers' pocketbooks. Rather, they continue to do things to keep their customers loyal. They continue to introduce new ideas, new products, new services, new delivery methods, new marketing ideas. They do it in multiple areas of the value-added chain to make it hard for imitators. And, most important, they constantly seek to reinforce the critical bond with customers.

How Department Stores Managed the Past

Take your eyes off customers and anything can happen. They stop coming around. They find a way to bypass you. They label you passé.

This is what happened to the big department stores.

For years, the department store was *the concept* that most appealed to consumers. Their size and purchasing power subjugated suppliers and generated expansion capital for still more stores. By the 1960s department store chains and holding companies had become multibillion-dollar corporations.

But somewhere along the line, many department stores began to manage the past. They were addressing a target group that had joined the endangered species list: housewives with lots of time on their hands.

New retailing forms arose, notably the discount store. Little by little, the discounters started chipping away. First they took the hard goods. Department stores countered by emphasizing apparel, soft goods and gift items. It wasn't enough. Once-proud Gimbels disappeared without a trace. Indiana's flagship department store, Robesons, fell with a thud. Chicago's Fairstore closed its doors. Other chains, notably Bonwit Teller, Bloomingdale's, Saks Fifth Avenue, are either bankrupt or for sale. Others, like Macy's, face a draining debt repayment schedule.

The biggest department store of all, Sears, is in trouble today because it stopped managing the future. Once the provider of convenience and unprecedented choice to customers in isolated areas who previously had no access to material goods, Sears grew with the nation. But by the mid-1970s, the company had begun to lose its appeal as a one-stop shopping emporium. It lost its core middle-class customers to those specialty stores that were cropping up in shopping malls all over America, stores with names like The Gap and The Limited and Benetton. Sears lost appliance business to stores like Circuit City, Silo and Highland Superstores and to discounters like K Mart, Target and Wal-Mart. It lost its toy department to Toys "Я" Us.

To be sure, Sears is now trying to make a comeback.

It has taken many bold steps recently to win back the customer, strategies we'll discuss later in this book. But the point is this: Sears lost the loyalty of its customers. Once you lose your customers' loyalty, it's hard to get it back.

How Holiday Inns Managed the Past

Holiday Inns faces the same problem as Sears. It, too, assumed that it could count on customers doing tomorrow what they did yesterday. Yet it was once a stellar example of managing the future, a classic story of American innovation.

Kemmons Wilson, a successful thirty-eight-year-old Memphis home builder, went on a family vacation in 1951. He hated the poor service he received from the musty mom-and-pop motels along the way—motels that charged extra for each of his children. So Wilson decided to build a better motel. By 1953, he had built four Holiday Inns, one on each highway coming into Memphis. And Wilson had the good sense to take the concept nationwide thereby inventing the future of motel franchising. Soon the Vegas-bright, fifty-foot-high "Nation's Innkeeper" signs were sprouting up along interstate highways at the rate of one every two and a half days. By 1968, when Holiday Inns opened its one thousandth facility, the company was bigger than its two nearest competitors combined.

Throughout the 1960s, Holiday Inns kept close to its customers. In 1965, it pioneered the first computerized reservations system. A nice touch. One of many.

Then something changed. Holiday Inns began to take its eyes off the customer while its top team tried to turn the company into a conglomerate. By the early 1970s, the company owned an ocean freighter, a dinette maker, a catering service, a bus service, a campground chain, a meatpacking company and an industrial park. While the company had its eyes off its customers, the oil cartel of 1973 hit, forcing motorists off the road and Holiday Inns into a tailspin.

Adding to its woes, an army of imitators came along and began building motels right next to Holiday Inns. New motels sprang up with names like Days Inn and Motel 6 for the budget-minded, and Marriotts and Hyatts for the business traveler.

On and on the market segmenting went, leaving Holiday Inns boxed in the moribund middle market. Like Sears and thousands of other firms both big and small, Holiday Inns lost the future when it stopped living and changing with the customer.

Managing the Future

So much for the perils of managing the past. Now let's look at the rewards that come from managing the future. The success formula isn't hard to understand: It is simply to stay close to the customers. Really close. Minute-to-minute close.

The companies profiled in *In Search of Excellence* were lauded for being "close to their customers." Yet fourteen of the forty-three got whamoed. What this means isn't that authors Peters and Waterman chose the wrong companies, or that companies like Levi Strauss, Texas Instruments, Atari, Avon, Tupperware, Wang Labs, Kodak, K Mart, Fluor and others weren't listening. What it means is that they weren't listening *enough*—not for the new era of turbulence that dawned at roughly the time *Excellence* was being researched.

*How Quality Inns
Manages the Future*

I once asked Robert Hazard, president of Quality Inns
International, how his company got the idea to segment
the chain.

Hazard laughed as he told me the story. While getting
a haircut in Phoenix, he asked the barber, "Where do
you go on vacation?" The barber responded that he and
his wife liked to drive to Las Vegas or San Francisco or
Southern California on their annual two-week trip. "And
where do you stay?" asked Hazard.

On the open road, we just pull into a budget motel,
responded the barber. But when we get to the big city
we splurge on a swanky downtown hotel. "My wife likes
to be where the action is," he explained.

Robert Hazard got out of that barber chair with a
little less hair and a lot more insight into his industry.
He realized that he'd never get this man's business. On
the open road, his motels were too expensive. In the
big cities, he was too cheap. As a result of this insight,
Quality pioneered market segmentation by an existing
hotelier in the early 1980s. While sprucing up its Quality Inns for the middle-budget market, the company
introduced Comfort Inns and Sleep Inns for the budget-
minded and Clarion Hotels to compete with upscale hotels.

Bob Hazard is a trend watcher par excellence. There
is a small box on his desk labeled "Lodging Trends."
Every time he hears or reads something significant, he
makes a note and puts it into the box, which he reviews
periodically. This is a simple discipline, but Hazard is
singularly devoted to trend-spotting. He realizes that
before you can ride the trends, you have to understand
them.

How McDonald's Manages the Future

In my corporate seminars, I often ask executives to name the most future-focused fast-food company. McDonald's invariably gets the most votes. I then challenge them to break up into teams and list as many "McInnovations" as possible.

They usually get the product innovations—the Big Mac (1968), the Egg McMuffin (1973), Chicken McNuggets (1983), the McDLT (1985), salads (1987) and the McChicken sandwich (1989)—but they often miss how McDonald's has ridden the changes in American society. For example:

- noticing more single people and two-career couples, McDonald's opened for breakfast.
- sensing Americans' desire for speed and convenience, McDonald's not only introduced one of the first drive-through windows, but also introduced a second window where patrons could pay. It issued headsets to workers assigned to the windows.
- anticipating the baby bust and the growing shortage of youthful workers for its counter positions, McDonald's started the McMasters Program and began actively recruiting older workers.

We could go on with this list, but you get the idea. McDonald's does what any business can learn to do: systematically respond to a changing external and internal environment with new products, services and ways of doing business.

Why Managing the Future Means Changing the Rules

Frank Perdue changed the rules in the poultry business. Before Perdue came along, chicken was a commodity product. It was found in the frozen food section, pale white, hard as a rock, with no brand name. Then Perdue developed a new breed of big-breasted chicken that he fed a diet of corn and marigold petals to bring out a healthy yellow color.

Then he redesigned the distribution system. Instead of delivering freezer-burned birds to distribution centers for later shipment to stores, he bought a fleet of trucks to take his chickens directly to supermarkets. That way his product could be kept fresher than commodity poultry.

Next he put a brand name on his packaging, and he advertised.

What was the customer's response? It turned out that if the customer was given a choice between a rock-hard, pale white commodity and a plump yellow Perdue chicken, many would choose Perdue. Perdue's premium poultry is typically priced a third higher than the commodity price, yet he has become one of the biggest producers in the nation.

Companies that manage the future strive to understand their customers better than the competition. Then they use that knowledge to provide greater satisfaction and choice. Along the way they often change the rules of the game.

Why Managing the Future Means Introducing Constant Improvements

We are a nation hooked on the "new and improved." If you don't believe it, just look at how often those three words are used in advertising. Does it make a difference in consumer purchases? It certainly does. Marketers use them over and over because they work.

Customers want the cutting edge. They have been

conditioned to accept nothing less. Customers expect more of your business today than they did yesterday.

Unless you keep introducing further improvements, they are apt to stray. Companies that manage the future pay constant attention to the innovation process. They know they can never stop looking for ways to improve if they want to stay ahead.

Why Managing the Future Means Meeting Customers' Needs

"Customers' needs" is a moving target. As soon as you figure out the riddle, it's time to come at it again with fresh eyes. Complacency leaves your company vulnerable.

If any product is stable, unaffected by the vicissitudes of change, it should be motor oil, right?

As it turns out, even motor oil producers must change with change. For ten years, Quaker State was the leader. In 1986, the company earned $50 million on revenues of $927 million. The following year, the company's fortunes suddenly changed for the worse. Market share fell from 22 percent to 18 percent. Quaker reported its first-ever loss of $45 million. Rival Pennzoil was the new king of the road. Its market share shot up from 18 percent to 23 percent.

The change? Quick-lube shops had begun to favor Pennzoil. The reason: Quaker was designed for big, low-RPM auto engines. Pennzoil was designed for smaller, hotter-running engines. Quaker State was making a product for a declining market, while Pennzoil had designed oil for today's automobile. To its credit, Quaker pioneered the plastic, easy-pour container, allowing the customer greater convenience. Then Pennzoil did one better. It came along with a square plastic container, which packed better and fit tighter on retailers' shelves.

Quaker was run over by the competition because it became content with managing the status quo. The challenge is always where your customers are going, not where they were yesterday.

Attackers vs. Defenders

So far we've seen that you must know how to manage the future if you hope to prosper in the face of the ten Driving Forces. You need another skill as well. You need to cultivate the mind-set of an attacker.

In his book *Innovation: the Attacker's Advantage*, Richard Foster shows how numerous companies were devastated because they underestimated the strength of a competitor's attack. Foster limited his analysis almost exclusively to technology-based companies. He shows how, for example, NCR was crippled in the early 1970s because it hung on to its electromechanical cash registers in the face of IBM's new electronic registers.

In this book, I have made liberal use of Foster's metaphor, but have not limited my analysis to technology-based companies. Instead, I have analyzed all types of businesses that have been successful attackers in recent years—high-tech and low-tech and no-tech, service and manufacturing, large and small. What was the advantage they offered customers? Why were their thrusts so powerful?

In the 1990s a competitive attack can come, not just from superior technology, but from a superior understanding of the forces of change. The attacker's advantage may in fact be a new technology. But it could just as well be a new way of doing business that promises greater speed, such as overnight parcel delivery or one-hour prescription lenses. It could be a new way of arranging a business that makes things more convenient for the customer, the way the quick-lube industry and mail-order companies have done.

Or the attack could come from offering the customer a new level of quality, as Mrs. Fields Cookies did. It could even be the introduction of deep discounting, as Price Club did, or a combination of two Driving Forces as Circuit City did with discounting *and* customer service.

Attackers enter and exploit markets where there are inefficiencies, where the existing players are complacent. They give the customer a new or a superior choice.

Defenders are often blind to the threat. Busy managing the day-to-day operations, they don't notice what's going on until it's too late. Too focused on their own internal procedures, they fail to grasp the external shifts that will soon clobber them.

HOW TO USE THIS BOOK

Managing the Future is based on my decade-long experience as a consultant to, and researcher of, American business. The book also taps my in-depth interviews with dozens of CEOs and leaders of future-managing companies. Some, like Rubbermaid, McDonald's, Wal-Mart, Liz Claiborne, American Airlines, Marriott, ARCO and Price Club are widely known. Others, while not household names, provide excellent examples readers will identify with and learn from. My work focuses on listening to America's leaders and finding patterns in how they think and act, and how they manage to be, to paraphrase an advertising slogan, "just slightly ahead of their time."

My purpose in writing this book is to share those patterns with you, to give you a framework in which to "hold" change in your mind as you go about leading your business into the future. Each of the chapters begins with an explanation of a Driving Force, so you can understand how it fits into the bigger picture.

But I haven't stopped with theory. Each chapter also has plenty of real-life examples. These examples show how certain companies got caught managing the past, and what happened to them as a result. They also show how other companies rose to new heights by managing the future. But ultimately, the principles and the examples don't matter if you can't translate them into action. That's why I end each chapter with action-oriented tips and techniques you can use to start changing your business for the better.

This book will be of greater value to those who see themselves as leaders rather than as "managers." It is a book for those who believe in the power of ideas and in action. Leaders do not fear change, they embrace it. Leaders use change as a stepping-stone, instead of allowing it to be a stumbling block; and leaders develop their skills in proactively anticipating, thinking through and creatively responding to change. The winners in the 1990s will be those individuals, no matter what business they are in, who can not only *envision* a future for their organizations, but who *make that vision a reality.*

I encourage you to read this book during a creative time in your schedule. Take it along on your next cross-country flight and read it with a cold drink and the bright sky out the window. Or take it with you on a weekend getaway. But don't try to read it at your desk with the phone ringing off the hook and people poking their heads in asking questions. Instead, read it when you are refreshed and in the mood to think about the future of your business and your career.

My suggestion is that you read it with your favorite tool for "downloading" ideas ready at hand, whether that be a dictating machine or a simple but effective idea notebook. Record ideas and future possibilities as soon as they come to mind.

But don't delay. Remember—if you don't take the time to understand these forces, your competitors will. Count on it. Somewhere out there someone is scheming to put you out of business. Your best defense is to get there first.

And one of the best ways to get there first is to take advantage of the Speed Imperative. For more about this important Driving Force and how you can cash in on it, turn to the first chapter.

SPEED

Exploiting the "FedEx" Imperative

First, there was the Federal Express Revolution, where you had to have everything overnight. Now, we've reached the point where we can't even tolerate that.

> —MARK WHITE
> Attorney
> Birmingham, Alabama

Doing it fast forces you to do it right the first time.

> —JOHN YOUNG
> CEO, Hewlett-Packard

Our whole business is built on speed.

> —TOM MONAGHAN
> Founder, Domino's Pizza

Time could end up being to the '90s what money was to the '80s.

> —*Time*

WHY MAKE SPEED the first of the ten Driving Forces? Because speed is a number one concern of Americans in the nineties—and, therefore, a number one opportunity for businesses that learn how to exploit it.

In this chapter, we'll start by examining how and why speed has become so crucial. I think you'll be surprised by how much things have changed in just the last decade. Then we'll see how speed is already at work in the marketplace, using three well-known industries as examples. As you'll find out, the Speed Imperative has rocketed certain future-managing firms to the top, while crushing companies that ignored it. At the end, I'll pass along eight steps you can take to make speed work to your company's advantage.

WHY AMERICANS VALUE SPEED

Why is speed one of the ten Driving Forces of change for the nineties? Put simply, it's because of the changing role of time in our lives.

In a survey for *The Wall Street Journal,* four out of ten people reported that their pet peeve was waiting in line while other cash registers stayed closed. More people mentioned waiting than even such aggravations as "solicitations using prerecorded messages," or "being quoted one price, then learning the real price is higher," or "getting a sales call during dinner."

Waiting in line is but a symbol of a larger issue—the growing importance of time.

This was supposed to be the leisure society. All the labor-saving products—self-cleaning ovens, wash-and-wear fabrics, computers, microwave ovens—were supposed to give us more time to relax. That's what futurists predicted, anyway. In 1967, testimony before a Senate subcommittee indicated that by 1985 people could be working just twenty-two hours a week or twenty-seven weeks a year or could retire at thirty-eight.

It hasn't worked out that way. A study by SRI International holds that nearly one third of all Americans belong to "harried households." One of the biggest changes causing the time crunch is the rise of the two-income family. Household chores used to be tackled by housewives—taking the kids to the doctor, making lunches, shopping, dealing with the plumber. But the spread of the dual-income family has eliminated the leading errand runner. In one study, 50 percent of dual-income respondents agreed with the statement: "Shopping and service tasks add stress to my life." Another question asked for reactions to the statement "We have less time to get our shopping done than five years ago." Sixty-six percent of dual-income respondents and 42 percent of single-income respondents agreed.

In addition, there are more single heads of households, divorced individuals, and those who never married. Because they often have no one to share household duties with, time-consuming responsibilities fall on their shoulders. Save them time, offer them more convenience, and you increase their loyalty.

The changing composition of American households is only part of the reason people feel time-starved. Another factor: rising complexity in the workplace. Simply keeping up with the information explosion takes up more of our time. As organizations have made it a goal to run lean on staff, workers in many business settings now regularly stay on the job longer and even work on weekends to catch up. Surveys by pollster Louis Harris and Associates show that the work week of Americans has been growing. It jumped from 40.6 hours in 1973 to 47.3 hours in 1984 and to 48.8 hours in 1987. In addition, the pollster discovered that small-business people now work more than fifty-seven hours a week on average, while professional people and those with incomes over $50,000 work more than fifty-two hours per week.

Whether or not they actually work as many hours as they report, the fact is, people are doing more these days.

"Their schedules are more ambitious," offers John Robinson, a University of Maryland researcher in how Americans use their time. We are taking more business trips and attending more conferences to keep up with change. We are schlepping the kids hither and yon to give them a variety of experiences. Partly as a result of this added complexity, Harris reports the average American's leisure time has declined by 32 percent since 1972, down from 17.7 hours per week to 8.5. (Harris defined leisure as totally free time, as distinguished from preparing for work, commuting, doing chores, attending classes, and so forth.)

The Bottom Line on Speed

Speed is not a new imperative. Americans have always valued efficiency. We are the nation that invented fast food, one-hour dry cleaning, and instant coffee. We look at those endless bureaucratic lines in Communist countries with pity. "How can people put up with such inefficiency?" we ask. What is different today is the extent to which customers are unwilling to tolerate wasted time. Although the Speed Imperative has always been around, in recent years it has gained the power to make or break a business.

Saving people time can become a competitive advantage if you exploit it. To put it simply, customers gravitate to businesses that value their time. Therefore, speed—speed of transaction, speed of repair, speed in responding to changing demographic or lifestyle needs of customers, or speed in responding to new demands— is a factor in the customer's decision of whom to patronize. In every area of your business there is a "fulfillment float" where the customer waits on you and not the other way around. Cut it by 10 percent or more relative to your closest competitor, and you have a strategic edge.

HOW SPEED IS AT WORK IN THE MARKETPLACE

We've seen how time and speed are becoming dramatically more important to Americans. This continuing trend has already forced many companies to adapt. Witness:

- By significantly reducing development time, General Electric slashed the time it takes to make and deliver a custom circuit breaker box from three weeks to three days.
- Motorola once required three weeks to turn out electronic pagers. Now it takes two hours.
- Hewlett-Packard used to take four and a half years to develop a new computer printer. Now it takes less than two years.
- It has traditionally taken four to six weeks for approval of home loan applications. During the rush to refinance in the 1980s, it sometimes took even longer. Citicorp Mortgage Inc. responded by launching the MortgagePower program, which sought to cut the approval time to two weeks. In early 1989, the company went further with MortgagePower Plus, which sought to give an electronic loan approval within an incredible fifteen minutes. The program has established electronic links between about 4,000 member realtors, mortgage brokers and lenders to achieve the speed break. Home buyers can sit down with their realtor and find out immediately if they qualify for their dream home. "The system is a quantum leap into the future for us," brags a Citicorp official. "It's been a big success already."

Why are such programs so successful? The issue is one of control. The self-employed person who puts in fifty-seven hours a week at work does so by choice. That same individual, put on hold by your receptionist, or forced to wait three weeks for delivery of a product, has another choice—where else to do business. Next time, instead of waiting in your line, that customer might order from a catalog. The delay in receiving may be a week or more, but the task itself is accomplished right away.

Look around. Observe how the speed issue is influencing the fate and fortunes of businesses. The winners are often the ones who speed up the satisfaction of a request.

Domino's Pizza is an obvious beneficiary. Tom Monaghan, the chain's peripatetic founder, was managing the future when he began offering not only the convenience of home delivery, but also the guarantee of speedy delivery. Domino's promises a $3 discount if delivery takes longer than thirty minutes. With this time guarantee, the chain has made speed and convenience—rather than the quality of the pizza—the cornerstones of its business. Other pizza-makers have been forced to scramble to try to match that guarantee, while Domino's has carved out a competitive niche in the minds of customers. Result: Almost unheard of at the beginning of the 1980s, it is now America's second-largest pizza chain.

In a moment, we'll look at ways to exploit the Speed Imperative. But first let's consider how three industries have been changed by this Driving Force. Their lessons apply to all of us.

The Eyeglass Industry

Nowhere in the medical field has speed become a more pronounced competitive advantage than in the eyeglass industry. Traditionally, optometrists and ophthalmologists had this field to themselves. The customer went for an eye exam, then chose from the physician's usually limited selection of lenses. The physician then sent the order to an off-site laboratory for fabricating. Days or weeks later, the customer was notified to come in and pick up the new glasses.

That began to change in 1966 when innovators Robert Hillman and Larry Kohan opened Hillman/Kohan, a prescription lens superstore in Saddle Brook, New Jersey. They were managing the future by anticipating customers' needs for greater speed and convenience. At Hillman/Kohan, the customer was examined by a staff optometrist, then allowed to choose from a wide array of in-stock frames. A staff optician ground the lenses and installed them in the frames, often within one hour. It was a revolutionary concept, and one that immediately caught on.

By 1971, Hillman/Kohan had fifteen stores in the New Jersey–Long Island area (later sold to Pearle Vision Center) and the concept had begun to spread nationally. By 1988, according to estimates by the American Optometric Association, 30 percent of the $10 billion spent on corrective lenses each year was spent at superstores and chain outlets. Not only have the superstores revolutionized product delivery, they've put time pressure on traditional providers of eye wear as well.

The impact on traditional optometrists has been acute. Many have forgone private practice for salaried work at the chains. Since sole practitioners can't match the superstores' wide selection, price advantages and the fast one-stop convenience, they will have to seek other competitive advantages, most notably personalized service and differentiation on the basis of quality. But there's no denying that speed has become an important new component of the eyeglass industry.

Parcel Delivery

In 1971, Federal Express revolutionized the parcel industry with its overnight delivery guarantee. Fred Smith, a twenty-eight-year-old ex-Marine, was managing a family-owned aviation company in Little Rock, Arkansas.

He continually got requests from area businesses to charter his planes for urgent delivery of packages. By sensing an unfilled and growing need, Smith created a whole new market based on the Speed Imperative.

That's not the end of the story. Federal Express's original time commitment to its customers was noon the next day. But because Federal Express continued to exploit the Speed Imperative, it did not stop there. To do so would have been managing the past. In 1982, it upped the ante on a growing pack of competitors and shortened its delivery commitment to 10:30 A.M. Two years later it offered a money-back guarantee. In 1985, it pioneered an innovative bar code system that allowed it to track a customer's parcel within thirty minutes of inquiry. Federal Express has indeed continued to change with change, and has changed the parcel delivery industry along with it.

Photo Processing

In 1980, Eastman Kodak surveyed American camera owners to find out if they wanted their color film developed in one hour instead of one week. Fewer than 5 percent said they did, and Kodak pursued the issue no further.

Soon thereafter came the one-hour minilab boom. Rooted in a new technology which allowed on-site developing, the phenomenon was a quick hit with time-constrained consumers. Unheard of before the late 1970s, minilabs, with names like Moto Photo, Fox Photo, KIS Photo and many others, continued to gain market share throughout the 1980s. By 1990, 20,000 minilabs had snapped up almost 40 percent of the $4.8 billion photoprocessing market.

Clearly, the Driving Force of speed has transformed

the photofinishing industry. Traditional processors, who once took their time developing pictures, have had to speed up or die. And the drive-up film kiosks have been big losers. Their market share dropped from 11 percent in 1983 to 2.5 percent in 1988. The best known of the kiosk operators, Fotomat, had to close dozens of the familiar, brightly colored kiosks that were its trademark. Its surviving kiosks are clustered around centrally located one-hour processing centers, designed to give customers the convenience of drive-up drop-off as well as speed close to that of the one-hour processors.

Traditional developers that did not improve turn-around time lost the battle to minilabs. The number of wholesale processors—companies that provide developing services to retailers—dropped from more than 400 in 1980 to 150 ten years later. The decline has come despite the fact that minilabs are more expensive than traditional photofinishers (about 6 percent on average). Clearly many consumers are willing to pay more for speed.

Because minilabs gave a segment of the picture-taking population something new—greater speed—they proliferated so rapidly in a single decade that the market may be nearing saturation. Moreover, increasing numbers of drugstores, food markets, discount department stores and superstores are now getting into the act by installing their own minilabs right in their stores. Because the challenge of managing the future is always looking for what's next, smart minilab owners are differentiating themselves with value-adding services such as two-for-one deals, portraits, video transfer and passport photos.

Has the one-hour developer neutralized speed as a source of competitive advantage? Not yet. Already, some minilabs are developing pictures in less than an hour. In Japan, a third of minilabs already offer processing in less than thirty minutes, while 75 percent offer processing in forty-five minutes or less. As the competition becomes more heated and the technology improves, units offering faster speed will continue to appear.

As minilabs continue to reduce the fulfillment float, it's important to note how swiftly they have already changed the customer's perception of waiting time—and the fortunes of businesses that did not respond quickly enough.

HOW TO WIN CUSTOMERS WITH SPEED

Eyeglasses, parcel delivery and photo developing are just three examples of how speed is transforming entire industries, creating new winners and losers in its wake. This Driving Force will continue to jump, brushfire-like, to other industries, regions, localities and markets. Perhaps to yours. How are you responding? What follows are eight steps to exploit the Speed Imperative in your business.

Step 1: Decide if Speed Is an Issue

I doubt the typical diner at a white-tablecloth restaurant will ever value speed. Fine dining is a "tempo business," one where the customer is time-conscious only if the pacing and timing are off. In some businesses, speed is anathema, whereas tempo is critical to customer satisfaction. Such businesses should not adopt the Speed Imperative as a competitive strategy.

But many other organizations have begun to cash in on the power of speed. Fast-food restaurants are an obvious example. Increasingly, other food establishments besides those in the fast-foods category have begun to exploit the Speed Imperative. Denny's, a family restaurant chain, rolled out its advertising campaign "Your meal in 10 minutes or it's free" in 1989. In part, this was a reactive move by Denny's because it must compete in many areas with fast-food restaurants and buffet-style concerns where the customers' perception of speed is greater.

The definition of what is "fast" or "timely" or "prompt" is definitely influenced by the customers' expectations. In fine dining, customers don't want speed, they want appropriate tempo. Ask yourself if your customers value speed. If the answer is yes, use the remaining steps in this chapter to shape a speed-based strategy.

Step 2: Challenge Time-Based Assumptions

Future-managing leaders are sensitive to the way in which their customers perceive speed.

Most organizations are ingrained in "that which exists"; they don't continue to charge the gates of "that which could be." "That which exists" might be defined in your business as "everybody knows it takes two weeks to do *x.*" Then along comes someone from outside who challenges this assumption. When that happens, everybody is dragged (kicking and screaming) into the future, which gradually becomes "the way things are."

In the furniture industry, "that which exists" might be how long it takes for the dealer to deliver a sofa after the customer has selected the style and fabric and ordered it. The customer expects that such a customizing procedure will take more time. But if sofa factory A can do the above in three weeks while sofa factory B takes three months, sofa factory A has an exploitable competitive advantage.

The field of medicine has long considered itself "above the fray" on the issue of speed. Two key assumptions dominate the thinking of the vast majority of medical practices: 1) There is no way to schedule appointments so that customers are spared long delays, and 2) The medical professional's time is more valuable than the customer's.

A few pioneering physicians have made mincemeat out of both of these assumptions. One of them is Neil Baum, M.D., a New Orleans urologist and speaker on physician marketing issues. Dr. Baum refers to his waiting room as a reception room and sees patients within twenty minutes of their appointment or he doesn't charge for the visit. The secret, Dr. Baum believes, is what he calls "informed scheduling." He trains his staffers to know how long to allow for various procedures.

The future lies in reducing the float between the customer's purchase decision and the satisfaction of that request, whether it's an oil change, completion of a new warehouse or delivery of a new sofa.

Take a mental inventory of all the places in the request-through-fulfillment cycle your customers experience. Then pick out the most time-consuming area for immediate action. Get your associates involved in brainstorming ways to reduce the amount of time this procedure or step takes, and implement the best suggestions.

Step 3: Poll Your Customers, but Listen to Your Instincts

Earlier, we saw how Kodak's research in 1980 found that only 5 percent of customers valued speed in photo processing. And then, shortly thereafter, came the minilab revolution.

The lesson is not that Kodak's research methods weren't so hot. Rather, it's that *customers often don't know what they want until they see it.* Yes, you should aggressively listen to your customers. But no, you should not expect them to gift wrap solutions for you—or even to appreciate your innovations until they've tried them out.

A better tactic: Ask customers where and how delays affect their satisfaction. Then look for ways speed can increase that satisfaction, and trust your instincts if you think you've come up with a bold new idea.

Step 4: Measure the Time between Request and Satisfaction

Whether it's a customer's request for product delivery or a journalist's request for information from your public relations department, you're being judged all the time. Measuring the average time elapsed from request to satisfaction will make you and your associates more responsive to the time issue, and will stimulate everyone to experiment with speed innovations.

There are two important categories of speed in business: manufacturing speed and speed to the customer. In manufacturing businesses, speed involves complex factors, all of which must come together if the widget is to roll off the assembly line. In service businesses, the "product" is manufactured on the spot, as when a front-desk clerk checks you in to the hotel. Although our discussion in this chapter focuses primarily on speed of satisfying the customer, manufacturing speed is another equally powerful source of competitive advantage.

Rudyard Istvan, vice president of The Boston Consulting Group, is a leading proponent of what is often called "time-based strategy." Istvan believes that in the future, speed, even more than cost or quality, must be the "over-arching management objective which subsumes the others." When the organization focuses on cycle time, Istvan believes it is forced to mesh previously uncoordinated activities and programs, such as cost-containment, quality and innovation.

"The greatest potential for reducing delays," writes Istvan, "almost always lies in processes that involve the most personnel. All too often, business cycles are viewed as a linear series of discrete, equally important tasks, each performed by a specialist. This overspecialization leads to multiple sign-offs, duplication of effort, mismatched inputs, and delays in reaching agreement. Time-based competitors look for ways to speed up repetitive tasks, isolate bottlenecks and analyze systems based on the idea of simultaneously occurring, parallel processes. As the organization is rearranged to allow rapid responses to change, the number of employees involved in each process will diminish.''

Istvan argues convincingly that this management philosophy can be applied everywhere in business. A full In basket in an executive's office is as much "work-in-progress inventory" as a bin of parts on the shop floor. There are fewer distinctions between manufacturing, service and office administration processes than many managers realize.

Regardless of where you set about collapsing the fulfillment float, you will see benefits accrue. The secret is to set standards for speed—then measure how you're doing against those standards.

Some examples: "All incoming calls will be answered before the third ring," or, "Exchange orders will be credited within three days of receipt," or, "All orders will be shipped within twenty-four hours of receipt."

Step 5: Let Customers Know What You're Doing

In 1990, Red Lobster restaurants launched a national program named Call Ahead Seating. This modified reservation system allows callers to obtain a number and a place in line before they leave home. Red Lobster's call-ahead program is hardly earth-shattering. But its test-marketing was so successful that Red Lobster trumpeted the inauguration of the program with national television advertising as well as in-house promotions.

When you make improvements that allow for faster service, be sure to let your customers know what you are doing. *Remember, an improvement doesn't have to be a revolutionary act—it can be an evolutionary act.*

Step 6: Offer More Speed to Those Who Will Pay for It

Offer premium service, even if you have to charge extra. Hertz launched its No. 1 Club Gold program in an effort to shave the time its customers spent claiming rental cars. Club Gold members fill out a single rental agreement upon joining and pay $50 per year. They can step off the plane and go directly to Hertz shuttle buses. These buses deliver them to covered parking areas, where their car is waiting with the trunk open, the engine running and the rental agreement hanging from the mirror.

"Some customers say it can literally take only five minutes from when they get off the plane to the time they hit the road," says Susan Donahue of Hertz. "It's actually exceeded our expectations."

For customers who are in a hurry, C&R Clothiers, a Los Angeles–based discount chain, offers Express Tailoring. For $15 extra, a man can pick out a suit at C&R and have it altered and ready to wear the next day—often by the next morning. Express Tailoring has been an unqualified success for the company. According to a company spokesman, "It's a major reason customers come to C and R."

Even if a new way of adding speed costs more, you'll find some customers willing to pay for it. Examine your request-through-fulfillment cycle and determine if there are bottlenecks than can be eliminated by passing the added cost on to the customer. Then, on a trial basis, check out the demand for such services.

Step 7: Reward Employees for Speed

Six days a week, planes from all over the country descend on Federal Express's main hub in Memphis. Every night at precisely 11:40 P.M., Federal Express's army of 4,000 part-time workers begins the task of unloading, sorting and reloading the planes. By 1:55 A.M., the job is complete and the planes begin to depart. All must be airborne shortly afterward to ensure they arrive at their destination cities in time for local couriers to deliver each package absolutely, positively, by 10:30 A.M. With service to 119 countries, speed is more than a value-added item for Federal Express. It is the very product the company sells.

For a while during the seventies, however, Federal Express had problems keeping its superhub running on time. How do you make employees care about customers they never see or talk to?

"We were having a helluva problem keeping things running on time," says Chairman Fred Smith. "We tried every kind of control mechanism that you could think of, and none of them worked. Finally, it became obvious that the underlying problem was that it was in the interest of the employees at the cargo terminal—they were college kids, mostly—to run late, because it meant that they made more money. So what we did was give them all a minimum guarantee and say, 'Look, if you get through before a certain time, you can go home early, and you will have beat the system.' Well, it was unbelievable. I mean, in the space of about forty-five days, the place was way ahead of schedule. And I don't even think it was a conscious thing on their part."

Smith understands a vital aspect to consistently delivering speed—involve all employees in the process by motivating them to perform. Are there ways you can restructure your company's compensation plan to directly reward speed?

Step 8: Offer Time Guarantees

Wells Fargo Bank offers to pay customers $5 in cash if they have to stand in line for more than five minutes.

Lucky's supermarket chain, faced with growing competition from convenience stores and fast-food outlets, now promises to open up additional lines if more than three people are waiting.

Do these types of promises really matter to customers? Count on it. As further proof, consider the overwhelming response tax preparer H&R Block received in 1990 when it rolled out its new Rapid Refund electronic filing program.

For an additional $25 the customer's tax return arrives at the IRS computer—instantly. A whopping 2.9 million customers opted for this speeded up service, of which one million were do-it-yourselfers who just wanted to speed things along. And for a small charge, those expecting refunds can opt to receive their money within days directly from H&R Block, rather than the several weeks the IRS can take. "We are convinced that Rapid Refund has helped differentiate us," observes Tom Bloch, president and CEO of the Kansas City–based chain. "It's allowed us to make a positive impression on our major competition—the do-it-yourselfers, who still account for 50 percent of all tax files."

Can you find ways to increase customer satisfaction by guaranteeing timely service? You may find that your program is a big hit also.

THE SURPRISING FRINGE BENEFIT
OF SPEED

The biggest downside of speed is the additional stress it supposedly brings on.

In fact, speed can actually improve employee morale, teamwork, cooperation, personal growth and pride in working for an "on-time machine" (as one airline puts it in its advertising). Companies studied for this book are already gaining competitive advantage from speed, and their people are proud to be associated with them.

If handled properly, doing it faster means doing it better, with fewer errors, greater synergy and coordination, which inevitably leads to greater customer satisfaction. Greater customer satisfaction leads to greater employee satisfaction as well. Federal Express drivers are in a business where speed counts, yet I've never experienced one of their drivers who seemed to be under stress because of job pressure. Most seem to like the tempo, because it is efficient, and because their customers respect them for keeping their commitments.

We've seen why speed is so essential to your future success, how it is already changing American industries and the steps you can take to get it on your side. The key point: To prosper in the next decade, you must rethink your relationship to speed. Above all, try something—now, right away.

Want to make the Speed Imperative even more powerful in your behalf? Here's how: Combine it with a higher Convenience Quotient. What's the Convenience Quotient and why is it so important to managing your company's future? Turn to the next chapter to find out.

DRIVING FORCE 2

CONVENIENCE

Creating Your Own "Domino's Effect"

If you don't make shopping easy for me, I'm not going to waste my time.

—MARLENE DASH
Corporate manager

Seventy-seven percent of U.S. homes now have the convenience of a microwave. What's now called cooking is more accurately described as assembling.

—Food product researcher

Even though I could go right around the corner to buy business supplies, it's easier to call an 800 number and place an order. They bring it right to the door.

—JOAN TEDESCHI
New York photographer

Our customer doesn't give a damn that we've been in business for twenty-five years. When she goes into a store she wants to see something new and she wants to see it now.

—LESLIE WEXNER
Chairman, The Limited

NOT LONG AGO I wanted to send a rocking chair to Texas. I'd promised to send a vintage World War II rocker, which had long been in our family, to my brother in time for the arrival of his firstborn child.

For weeks the reminder kept showing up on my things-to-do list. Then it dawned on me that I was putting it off because I didn't know how to accomplish the task. Should I crate it and call UPS? Would a moving company be more appropriate? A trucking line?

When I couldn't put it off any longer, I started doing research. Everyone I called confirmed my suspicions— this was going to be a hassle. My request was unusual. It didn't fit their way of doing things. Yes, they could do the job, but at their convenience, not mine. Finally, one freight company clerk told me about a company called The Packaging Store, which I called.

"Yes sir, we come out to your home, pick it up, crate it in our special packaging, ship it, deliver it—no problem," said the voice on the phone.

"Sold! How soon can you get here?" I exclaimed.

In today's complex world, we can never master everything, whether it's shipping a rocking chair to Texas or something a lot more complicated. That's where convenience comes into the equation.

Convenience is not a new Driving Force. Yet it is often underrated as a factor in business success. That's precisely why it can be your key competitive advantage in the 1990s. In this chapter we'll take a look at why convenience is so important, we'll observe how it is already transforming American industries and finally, we'll examine how you and your company can cash in on it.

WHY YOUR CONVENIENCE QUOTIENT IS SO IMPORTANT

In the eyes of customers, your business has a Convenience Quotient. If that quotient is high, the customer is more apt to do business with you. The customer calculates that quotient by dividing the desire for fulfillment by the hassle and annoyance that must be endured. Every time customers consider satisfying a need, they consciously or unconsciously calculate the Convenience Quotient.

The customer's desire to achieve satisfaction is mitigated by factors such as: "Is the business open when I have time to go?"; or, "Will I be able to figure out the directions that come with this product?"; or, "How much can I accomplish in one stop?" and so on. The result of the Convenience Quotient calculation is a decision of whether to buy from you or a competitor; whether to buy now or wait; whether to use your method of satisfaction or seek another.

So, here's the message: Businesses, products and services that have a low Convenience Quotient can count on losing customers to those that respond creatively to this Driving Force.

Why is convenience growing in importance? The previous chapter examined how the time crunch is forcing Americans to look for ways to get more done in less time. Ditto convenience. And convenience is also an important way of differentiating your business. In a world of look-alike products and services, customers increasingly make buying decisions based on intangible factors such as convenience. According to one survey, seven out of ten customers who switch from one company to a competitor cite poor service—not price or quality. And three out of five people responding to a survey by Cambridge Reports, a research organization, said that "in choosing a service, cost is less important than having needs met."

Capitalizing on Convenience

Turning convenience into a source of competitive advantage begins with a mental shift. It requires that you observe your business anew from the customer's viewpoint. Everything—from your products and services to the environment in which they are purchased, to the after-sale servicing—must be re-examined from the standpoint of enhancing convenience. Consider the Convenience Quotient of shipping a rocking chair. The Packaging Store rated high because:

- It was full service. I didn't have to do any research to find out the different steps involved in shipping a large item.
- It was one-stop shopping. I could accomplish the task with a single phone call.
- It was customized. I could make an appointment for the pickup rather than waiting at home all day.
- It was personalized. I could deal with someone who seemed to care and who specialized in this service.
- It was a safe choice. I was made to feel secure that the package would arrive on time and in good condition.

In short, the Convenience Quotient in this transaction was so high that next time I have a similar need, I'll surely think of The Packaging Store right away. This national chain is but one example of the new businesses, services and products that have already responded to America's clamor for convenience. Already, the consumer can find everything from the now-common home-delivered pizza and mail-order catalog, to rent-a-car services that deliver and pick up the car and scores of personal service companies that will "find it, do it, wait for it." And yet, surprising as it might sound, this isn't enough. *The convenience you offer your customers today won't be enough to satisfy them tomorrow.* We're at the beginning of a convenience revolution. Only by continuously improving upon your Convenience Quotient can you stay ahead of the competition.

Staying on the Cutting Edge

Innovators like The Packaging Store have gained ground by adeptly responding to the Convenience Imperative. What they are doing for their customers represents the cutting edge . . . for the moment, that is. Although their achievements represent the cutting edge today, that edge is always advancing. The only way they can *continue to stay ahead* is to keep on coming out with improvements.

The dirty rotten truth is this: Customers are never satisfied with the status quo. Because they have so many choices, they don't have to be. Convenience is always in the eyes of the beholder, and today's beholders are influenced as much by convenience innovations *outside* an industry as within it. When Federal Express can guarantee to get a parcel to Dallas by 10:30 tomorrow morning, it affects the customer's perception of how long it should take to ship a rocking chair there.

Future-managing businesses don't wait for competition to force them to get better. They know that the best defense against attack is to constantly raise their Convenience Quotient by introducing improvements that discourage challenges. *Attackers obsolete their own products, services and ways of doing business.* They compete not so much with other businesses as with themselves, in a self-inspired quest to widen their lead.

Weighing the Costs

There are, of course, limits to the conveniences a business can provide. Convenience costs. But it also pays.

Unless it pays, it is not a source of competitive advantage. The attacker is always the one who figures out *how* to make it pay. The fact that it costs should never become a justification for leaving well enough alone. This is a trap businesses fall into which leads them to manage the past. "That would cost us too much to provide" is a common refrain in organizations that exhibit a lack of creative spark. The fact that it costs should never be allowed to overrule the possibility that a convenience innovation could be made to pay far more.

For decades, banks had "bankers' hours." They opened late and closed early, and never on weekends. So when future-focused banks began expanding their hours and opening Saturdays, the skeptics in the banking community crossed their arms and said, "That will cost them." But instead, what happened was that many of the banks who stayed open longer attracted more business as a result, more than paying for the increased operating costs of staying open.

The convenience of home-delivered pizza doesn't cost Domino's, it pays. Because of its "we deliver" distribution method, Domino's stores don't have to be in high-rent locations since the vast majority of their customers never see the pizza factory.

And so it goes. Convenience can actually increase profitability rather than raise costs. The attacker looks for ways to make convenience pay. The defender looks only at the cost of adding convenience innovations, and the inconvenience to himself of doing so.

Convenience innovations often pay for themselves because they stimulate demand. The evidence of this is everywhere. The availability of "goof-proof" Japanese cameras and video recorders, along with fast, convenient minilabs has stimulated picture-taking. The convenience and speed of overnight mail has increased the amount of packages that absolutely positively must get there overnight. The reality is that pent-up demand is caused not only by budgetary limitations, but also by time limitations. Increase the convenience of a product or service and you may also increase demand.

HOW CONVENIENCE IS AT WORK
IN THE MARKETPLACE

We've considered the growing importance of convenience and how it often pays for itself. Now let's turn our
attention to four industries in which companies have already learned this lesson—sometimes to their profit, and
sometimes to their pain.

The Quick-Lube Industry

The quick-lube industry provides an excellent example
of both winners and losers—those who raised the Convenience Quotient and reaped the rewards, and those who
managed the past and had to pay the price.

The industry did not even exist until the late 1970s. It
was "invented" by Jim Hindman, a former Baltimore
football coach. After becoming frustrated with the inconvenience of traditional auto dealers, Hindman launched
Jiffy Lube. The growth of his company and the industry
it leads is one reason service departments of auto dealers
have become money losers.

Convenience has not been a priority for auto dealers.
Their method of operation almost always requires the
customer to give up his vehicle for the entire day, even
if the actual service takes less than an hour.

It's easy to see how this system came to be. Like law-
yers, service departments sell their time. For this reason,
there was a strong *disincentive* to raise the Convenience
Quotient. Having the customer wait for repairs, however
minor, was "not the way we do things here." Not even
for simple oil changes, which newer cars must have every
5,000 miles.

Over time, customers changed; the dealers didn't.
Taking the car in for servicing was becoming more and
more of an inconvenience. More people joined the work

force in the seventies and eighties than ever before, and therefore needed their cars every day. But most dealers took the attitude that "That's not our problem, it's your problem. And besides, there is no solution to the problem even if we defined it as a problem."

Add to this the fact that after the Arab oil embargo of 1974, the number of service stations in the United States began to decline precipitously. In Southern California, for instance, gasoline station service bays decreased to about a fourth of their 1974 peak, down from 20,610 to 6,455, according to the Lundberg Survey, an industry clearinghouse.

Collectively, these conditions led to the rapid rise of the quick-lube industry, which by 1989 was worth $1.5 billion with over 3,800 shops across the United States. Innovation #1: no-appointment oil changes in ten to thirty minutes. Innovation #2: prices based on the service rather than the time, which gives both the service provider and the customer an incentive for speed and convenience.

Belatedly, some auto dealers are responding—not by rethinking any significant aspect of their modus operandi, but by trying to copy the quick-lube attackers. Ford and GM began experimenting with quick-lube departments on dealer premises. If the big two are successful, they may change customers' perceptions that dealership service is slow, costly and inconvenient. Had they responded to the quick-lube threat earlier, they might not have lost this portion of their business in the first place.

The Supermarket Industry

Like the auto dealers, for years the supermarket industry ignored the lifestyle shifts that were increasing the importance of convenience. Result: aptly named convenience stores, now over 50,000 in the United States, accounted for 7.1 percent of all grocery sales in 1987. At the same time, more and more Americans (45 percent by 1989) began to eat out at least once a day. Once a special occasion, eating out is now as common as cooking at home for millions of Americans.

"What's that got to do with us?" many grocers asked. Busy with the present, they failed to manage the future.

Not all of them, to be sure. The glowing exceptions include grocers like Giant Foods, a Washington, D.C.-area chain, which studied changing demographics and lifestyle trends and began brainstorming ways to ride the convenience wave. Giant was among the first to offer items such as gourmet meals-to-go, fresh pizza made at the store, delicatessens, salad bars and fresh cut flowers.

Giant Foods chose to be an attacker rather than a defender—and the profits followed. Those grocery stores that didn't respond, didn't survive. Of the grocery stores that closed in 1986, 64 percent were conventional supermarkets. The convenience store encroachment has taken its toll. While the number of convenience stores has doubled in the last decade, the number of supermarket chains has steadily declined.

The Telephone Industry

Telephone service is an example of society's drive for greater and greater convenience. In little more than a century, the telephone has evolved from a hand-cranked, wall-mounted device that only the wealthy could afford, to a ubiquitous communications medium.

Thousands of innovations have furthered its progress: touchtone phones, cordless phones, airplane phones and, of course, cellular or mobile phones. Related innovations have furthered the telephone's Convenience Quotient. The answering machine, now in one out of every three American households, and voice-mail make it possible to "time shift" the sending and receiving of messages. In addition, telephone lines can be used to send both computer data (via modems) and hard copy (via fax machines). The toll-free number, combined with the credit card, allows any business to become a national concern.

The future promises even more telephone conveniences: interactive cable TV programming, order- and pay-by-phone programming that will make video rental obsolete, and other services. (The added convenience of being able to preview movies and order videos by phone is something all video rental stores and services should be aware of now. If such a service is implemented, video stores could become an endangered species. Just as attendance at U.S. theaters declined after the introduction of the rental video and the low-cost VCR, video rental services could suffer if they don't look at new possibilities to offer their customers.)

But even with the telephone, a device that comes close to ultimate convenience, the cutting edge is constantly evolving. Listen to Craig McCaw, founder and chairman of Washington-based McCaw Cellular: "In the future, telephone numbers will be associated with people, not places. You won't have to be bound by a plug on the wall and a six-foot cord. People who call your phone number will be connected to you, wherever you happen to be." McCaw is working to make this vision a reality.

The Airline Industry

In his book *Moments of Truth,* SAS Airlines president Jan Carlzon describes the difficulty in getting people in an organization to think about convenience as experienced by the customer. When he took over the troubled airline, there was a product orientation that he had to change.

"As I learned more about SAS, I was amazed at how many policies catered to the equipment or to the employees, even if they inconvenienced the passengers. Equally amazing was how easy these practices were to spot and to rectify by looking at them from the point of view of our target customer: the frequent business traveler."

Arriving at Copenhagen airport on an SAS flight from New York, the new president had to change planes to get to Stockholm. Like many frequent fliers, Carlzon had hand baggage and was tired from flying all night. Once inside the terminal, he looked around the concourse for the Stockholm gate. He saw planes bound for Los Angeles, Chicago and Rio—but none for Stockholm. When Carlzon asked an SAS employee where the Stockholm gate was, he was told it was in concourse A—half a mile away!

"But why isn't it right here?" Carlzon asked. "All of us are going on to Stockholm." Eyeing the president with a slight air of superiority, the agent retorted, "Only wide-body planes park here."

Carlzon persisted. "You mean to say there are a lot of passengers here in Copenhagen who get off the plane from New York and then immediately board the plane to Chicago? Is that why all the wide-bodies are next to each other?"

"No, no," the agent answered. "They're here because they're all serviced at the hangar right over there."

Carlzon tried to explain how inconvenient the setup was, but he received little sympathy. The planes were positioned at the departure gate *that was most convenient for the employees rather than the customers.* Concluded Carlzon, "I've heard many a business traveler swear up and down about having to rush around between gates, but

I've never heard an airplane complain about being dragged a couple of hundred yards."

Needless to say, at the Copenhagen airport these days, SAS tows more planes from concourse to concourse and passengers do less walking between connections. Whereas two-thirds of SAS passengers used to change concourses at Copenhagen, that figure is now less than a third. "Not only are our passengers less harried," reports Carlzon, "but we've minimized delays caused by waiting for passengers who needed a few extra minutes to dash from one concourse to another."

HOW TO PROFIT FROM CONVENIENCE

Jan Carlzon faced what every future-oriented manager faces: the weight of the past; the weight of doing things "the way we have always done them"; the weight of doing things because it's easier for you, even though it's less convenient for customers.

Your associates can provide you with useful ideas on ways to add meaningful conveniences only after they understand the philosophy of being customer-driven. And how do you instill that philosophy? We've identified three key steps: 1) defining ultimate convenience, 2) taking a convenience audit, and 3) improving the purchasing cycle.

Defining Ultimate Convenience

What customers really want is to be able to access your offerings any time of the day or night, from anyplace, on their terms rather than yours. Of course, this ideal is impossible to achieve for most businesses. But that is not the thinking process out of which competitive advantages are born. That is not the thinking process that leads to managing the future. Instead, make the effort to visualize what the customer would really prefer. This is the best place to start the creative juices flowing. Later, you can work backwards to what is feasible.

Take a few minutes right now to think about what ultimate convenience might mean to your customer. Ultimate convenience is realized when your customer controls when, where and how your product or service is available. You've achieved it when you shift the locus of control totally and completely to your customers. A twenty-four-hour business shifts control of purchasing time to the customer. The business that takes phone orders shifts control of the purchase place and method.

Raising your Convenience Quotient starts in the perceptual realm. It begins by exploring a fundamental question: What are customers really after when they transact business with you? To see this transaction in a fresh light, walk in your customers' shoes through the entire process, from discovery of your business, to after-sale contacts. Try to forget the costs to you—that will come later. Focus on the impediments to immediate satisfaction. Chart out the steps to fulfillment. Ask, What is the ultimate in convenience for my customer?

Taking a Convenience Audit

Once you've defined an ultimate goal, you can further raise your convenience consciousness by "auditing" your business. Start by identifying areas where customers experience the most frustration. Next ask the question, Where is the opportunity in this problem that neither we nor our competitors have exploited? If your competitors have already exploited the problem, then you are acknowledging that you need to play catch-up.

Look at the various "moments of truth" your customers experience. Moments of truth are those crucial points of customer contact with a firm, its people, products and services. These moments begin as soon as a customer walks in the door. Is the purchasing experience as convenient as it could be? Do certain customer groups need more conveniences than others? Some retail businesses cater to parents with children by having in-store childcare facilities. If your business has a sizable constituency of senior citizens, what special services might you implement? Identify any negative moments of truth and brainstorm ways to make them positive. Consider the following questions:

- Are you constantly training and retraining your people to think about the customers' convenience rather than their own?
- Are employees—whether on the phone or in person—consciously thinking of the impression they make on the customer?
- Do you have enough knowledgeable staff to answer customers' questions immediately?
- Can customers achieve satisfaction of their needs with a minimum of contacts?
- Is it easy to get to the person in charge, in person, by phone or through the mail?
- Is the customer's after-sale experience handled as efficiently as the sale itself?

Part of your convenience audit should include customer thoughts, complaints and opinions. These serve as feedback and help you keep up on new trends.

Improving the Purchasing Cycle

Defining ultimate convenience and auditing your business are two profit-boosting methods that look at the big picture. Now I'd like to suggest a third way to cash in on convenience. This third idea requires you to focus narrowly on one key aspect of your relationship with customers and clients: the purchasing cycle. The future-focused manager must constantly seek ways to improve the Convenience Quotient at each step of the purchasing cycle, whether the customer is buying groceries or tax preparation services. The easiest way is to break down the purchasing cycle into six aspects:

1. The time frame
2. Payment methods
3. Ease of doing business
4. Ease of acquisition and return
5. Ease of use
6. After-sale service

Let's look at each one to see how convenience can be added for competitive advantage.

1. THE TIME FRAME

In the latter half of the 1980s, something happened to the shopping experience for many Americans—it ceased to be fun. With time at a premium, shoppers turned into purposeful hunters of goods and services. In 1982, consumers spent an average of ninety minutes per visit in shopping malls. By 1988, the average time per visit had dropped to sixty-eight minutes. What used to be a relaxing way to spend the afternoon has become a chore to finish as soon as possible.

"Once they've made a choice, they really want out of the store in a hurry," observes veteran retail consultant William Ress. "That's the biggest single area that retailers can improve in their operations."

Some businesses are doing just that. Kroger, the supermarket chain, is constantly exploring ways to get shoppers in and out more easily. For example, the company set up separate cash registers at both its salad bars and deli stands for take-out customers. Lucky Stores is challenging the long-standing assumption that grocery shoppers should be kept shopping as long as possible. In San Diego, shoppers can get in and out of its Advantage stores more conveniently because of design innovations borrowed from fast-food restaurants, upscale supermarkets and warehouse outlets. Aisles are wide and staples and frozen foods are located close to the checkout stands. Even 7-Eleven and the other convenience stores are experimenting with drive-in windows. Can you find ways to make the purchase faster for your customers?

2. PAYMENT METHODS

While dozens of water-bed dealers have closed their doors in recent years due to flagging demand, Bedroom One of Indianapolis has achieved a competitive advantage by introducing a convenient payment plan. Qualified buyers can take up to three years to pay for a complete bedroom set. The financing costs Bedroom One more, but the result, says co-owner Bev Nelson, is that customers invest in more expensive furniture because they can stretch out their payments.

While hardly a new strategy, introducing convenient payment methods stimulates demand. Forward-looking fast-food concerns have discovered this too. After a two-year test, Carl's Jr. became the first major chain to accept ATM cards. Early results indicate that using plastic induces a greater appetite: The cardholders spend an average of 50 percent more than those who pay cash.

By offering as many payment methods as possible—

cash, store and major credit cards, and local checks—a company can entice customers. One irony is that consumers can use credit cards to purchase everything from auto parts to weekly diaper service, but not for groceries. Vacationers are often out of luck since many grocers refuse out-of-town checks. Although supermarkets have expanded their offerings to include everything from floral arrangements to kitchen appliances, their customers can't pay for these items on credit. An obvious failure to keep up in convenience.

Why haven't grocery stores embraced plastic? Supermarket owners point to their slim margins and the fees credit card companies charge merchants. But future-managing supermarkets have figured out solutions. In Southern California, Mrs. Gooch's Natural Ranch Markets was among the first to accept credit cards. And others have begun to follow suit. Could you boost business by making it easier for your customers to pay?

3. Ease of Doing Business

The ultimate in convenience is approached when the seller brings his wares to the buyer, rather than the other way around. Alfred Dunhill was one of the first tailors to realize the power of the Convenience Quotient when he began selling suits to executives on the job. Instead of the busy executive taking time out to go to a tailor, Dunhill, whose top-of-the-line men's suits sell for $3,000, makes appointments with clients at their convenience, then brings along hundreds of swatches of fabric. Typically, the Dunhill tailor returns for two fittings.

Earlier in this chapter, we saw how Giant Foods achieves competitive advantage by constantly innovating new services. The future belongs to supermarkets that reinvent themselves not just as food emporiums but as one-stop service centers. The midwest's Hy-Vee Food Stores Inc., for instance, has installed not only prepared-food sections, but in-store shoe repair shops and laundries and is introducing new services, from full-service banks to travel agencies. In the years ahead, even baby-sitting services, home repair and poodle washes are possible, say company officials.

And what about the inconvenience of shopping in supermarkets that approach hypermarkets in size? In California, Vons Grocery Co. has already tackled that issue head-on by setting up a convenience store—with its own check-out system—inside a regular grocery store. The Vons Express Store stocks the same items found in 7-Eleven–type stores, but sells them at regular supermarket prices, typically about 20 percent below convenience store rates. In the future, customers may not even have to get out of their cars. At its Pasadena, California, store, Vons is experimenting with drive-up window service.

Make a list of the ways you can make it easier for customers to do business with you.

4. EASE OF ACQUISITION AND RETURN

The less effort the customer has to make, the more attractive that product becomes. This includes not only offering the service at a place that is more convenient for the customer (such as a branch bank), but also giving the customer the option to determine the place. Home delivery is the most obvious example of ease of acquisition. Charging extra for nonstandard delivery service (for people who don't own cars, for example) is certainly worth the effort. Ease of return is the problem of returning items, whether purchased in the store or by mail.

Availability is also part of ease of acquisition. Let's say you've chosen an item, and you're ready to buy, but the item is out of stock. You spent valuable time making your selection, but you're without the product. This is very important to many customers, even if the item is not needed immediately.

That's why half of each Circuit City superstore is devoted to warehousing ample units of the appliances and electronics they sell. Result: Customers almost always get immediate delivery, even during peak selling seasons, rather than having to wait for the store to order it.

Ease of return is closely related. It overcomes buying resistance because it increases customers' comfort level. Often, returning a mail-ordered item is so difficult and costly that consumers end up keeping products they don't want. Next time around, they're afraid to buy. Offering clear instructions and prepayment of the returned item is a convenience incentive to the consumer. In-store returns could be made more convenient by having a special service desk for such transactions and a liberal returns policy (reasonable number of days/no questions asked).

How can you improve the availability and ease of return of your products and services?

5. EASE OF USE

To achieve competitive advantage in this arena, everything from the product to its packaging must be reconsidered from the convenience perspective. Is your product easy to open and close? Easy to carry? Portability is a crucial criterion in our mobile society. Portable products allow the consumer to do two things at once. Product categories of the previous decade that used portability as their primary selling point include:

- Portable, single-serving desserts, such as the Dove Bar. According to the National Ice Cream Retailers Association, "frozen novelties" had sales of $2.75

billion in 1988 and are the fastest-growing segment of the frozen-food market.

- Laptop computers. Since Radio Shack introduced the first laptop in 1983, the number and availability of these go-anywhere PCs has steadily grown. Today there are over 100 different types of laptops available, made by more than ten different companies.

- Personal stereos. This product is not only portable, it's synchronous—it allows the user to do two things at once: walk, jog, run, read or whatever else. Sony, more than any other company, has exploited the Convenience Imperative with scores of lightweight, go-anywhere products.

- Audiotape and videotape instruction. These tapes, for everyone from doctors to teachers to salespeople, provide packaged updates and information that can be "consumed" anywhere. Although videotapes don't provide quite the synchronous aspect that audiotapes do, they make information more convenient because of the visual aspect.

How can you make your products and services easier to use?

6. AFTER-SALE SERVICE

All products and services can have problems. By planning ahead for these problems and arranging convenient ways to deal with them, your company can avoid dissatisfied customers. One of the easiest ways is to offer a toll-free customer service number or hotline. General Electric has gone to great lengths to show customers it cares. The GE Answer Center operates twenty-four hours a day, seven days a week with repair tips and help for owners who can't get GE products to work.

Additional ideas: fast replacement of defective items; easy return policies; free in-house servicing for large appliances or cars; immediate attention to errors in bank statements and tax preparation; and training seminars or tapes (for computer software, add-ons or upgrades).

What can your company do to make its after-sale experience more convenient for your customers?

Convenience. It's a Driving Force today that's well worth working on. Don't ignore this powerful weapon as you look for ways to keep your company focused on the future. And don't ignore the forthcoming Age Waves. As you will see in the next chapter, three powerful demographic changes are rushing through our economy, knocking down those companies that are not prepared.

AGE WAVES

Profiting from Three Generations

Seniors, today and in the future, want more than just cents-off discounts—they want an experience.
                                        —KEN DYCHTWALD
                                        Gerontologist and author

AMERICAN BUSINESS IN the 1990s will be rocked by three successive age waves: the mature market, the baby boom and the baby bust. These waves are growing stronger. They can swamp your company or, conversely, sweep it toward higher profits. Consider, by way of example, how the aging of the baby boom nearly left Levi Strauss high and dry.

Levi was riding high in the early 1970s when the baby boom turned blue jeans into an unofficial uniform. By 1980, the company's sales had mushroomed to $2.8 billion. Then sales fell off the table. By 1984, Levi Strauss had been forced to close twenty-two plants and lay off hundreds of workers. The reason: "The demographics have been against us," conceded chairman Peter Haas. But Levi managed to recover by refocusing on a maturing baby boom. Its line of Dockers slacks, styled for American males between the ages of twenty-five and forty-nine, has sold more than $300 million in four years. In 1989 the company had record sales of $3.6 billion.

DEFINING THE AGE WAVES

Let's quickly define the three key age waves of the nineties before we observe how some companies are already cashing in.

The Mature Market

The mature market, which consists of people over the age of fifty, is suddenly soaring. Everywhere, we see statistics like these:

- People over sixty-five are the fastest-growing segment of the U.S. population.
- People over fifty—25 percent of the population in 1990—are the most affluent consumer group in history. The fifty-plus age group controls two-thirds of the net worth of all U.S. households, and accounts for 40 percent of consumer spending.
- Eighty percent of all luxury travel in America is purchased by people over fifty-five.

The Baby Boom

No doubt about it, the progress of the baby boom generation has and will continue to capture the attention of marketers. For the most part, the baby boom is composed of the children of the mature market. As the 76 million Americans born between 1946 and 1964 move through the life cycle, they are like a pig in a python's stomach, comprising a third of the nation's population. The number of households headed by those between thirty-five and fifty-four will grow by 50 percent by the year 2000.

The Baby Bust

Hard on the heels of the boomers come the baby busters, those people born between 1965 and 1978. They are called busters because during the years they were born, there were so few of them being born that demographers refer to this period as a bust. This age wave is affecting American business by restricting the labor pool. Consider these effects:

- By the year 2000 the United States will experience a sharp decline in the twenty-to-twenty-nine age group, from 32 percent to 21 percent.
- In the next decade, the number of young workers entering the job market will shrink by as much as 10 percent.

AGE WAVES IN THE MARKETPLACE

How are these three age waves affecting the marketplace? By examining each one in turn, we can see how some companies are profiting and others are finding problems. With these real-world experiences under our belts, we can then turn our attention to formulating some rules for making the age waves pay off.

Serving the Mature Market

So far we've seen statistics about the burgeoning mature market. But what good are such statistics unless they are translated into viable products, services and methods that attract new customers? To the vast majority of businesses, catering to the mature market has been limited to offering senior discounts. Such discounts have long been expected—hardly a way to distinguish from all the rest.

Your knowledge of the senior boom is useless unless
you actually *do something with it* to change the way you
run your business, manage your employees, position
your company. Let's consider how several firms from
different industries have translated demographic data
about seniors into bona fide competitive advantages.

BARNETT BANK. Barnett Bank, a decentralized financial institution with 550 offices in Florida and Georgia,
launched its Senior Partners Program in 1982. Retired
residents hold an estimated three-quarters of Florida's
deposit funds, so going after the mature market wasn't
exactly a stroke of genius. The difficult part was listening
to these customers and then creating the right value-
adding services that truly raised satisfaction levels. Senior
Partners' amenities include: free checking; free travelers'
and cashiers' checks; a special statement that summarizes
all accounts held at Barnett's, including IRAs and CDs;
an accidental death insurance policy; brokerage services;
and a newsletter.

The cost of all this? It's free. Anyone over age fifty-five
with a Barnett checking account and investment account
can become a member. Senior Partners has more than
600,000 members, and the more than $8 billion in
deposits generated by the program represent a significant
share of the bank's $29 billion asset base and more than
40 percent of its retail deposits.

Barnett's early entry into the field allowed it to steal
a march on competitors. "We were very fortunate that
we entered marketing segments in 1981," observes
Judie MacDonald, vice president for retail sales at the
Jacksonville-based bank. "When we came out with Senior Partners, we were one of the first major banks to

introduce such a program. Not until the first quarter of 1985 did any of our competitors launch a similar program."

HILTON HOTELS. Hilton Hotels knew its Senior Honors program wasn't working. So the hotel company discarded the restrictions that made the program unwieldy and installed a whole range of new benefits designed to make its 300 worldwide hotels more appealing to seniors.

For an annual fee, anyone over sixty and retired persons over age fifty-five can receive:

- Up to 50 percent off room rates (the rates are the lowest published rates available and vary with each hotel).
- Dinner discounts of 20 percent at Hilton restaurants.
- A point system that allows frequent visitors to earn free nights at participating Hiltons.
- A variety of free services ranging from allowing a member's spouse to stay free, to use of hotel health clubs, to a morning newspaper.

Hilton launched a heavy promotion of its revamped Senior Honors. "It's drawn a lot of attention from seniors," says a spokesman. Fees are $25 for a domestic membership, $50 for a worldwide membership and $150 for a lifetime membership.

K MART STORES. What do seniors want? Sometimes just easier access. For instance, some K Mart stores are striving to make things easier for seniors with special store hours and transportation services, and by offering meals and meeting facilities for senior groups. K Mart's eye for the aging population has also brought changes in the merchandise mix. Clothes designed to appeal to senior citizens are more prominent. The cosmetics counter now carries makeup for older women. Even the sporting goods department has changed. It now has physical fitness equipment such as stationary bicycles and treadmills for active retirees.

H. J. HEINZ COMPANY. What seniors emphatically *don't* want is to be talked down to. Marketing to seniors is more complex and subtle than simply saying, "Hey, old folks, have we got a product for you." H. J. Heinz Company tried that approach a while back and came up short. The company believed that there was a market for baby-food-like meals for customers with bad teeth. But the elderly avoided the product, perhaps because they were too embarrassed to buy a product that called attention to their problem. More recently, the company discovered a way to appeal to the mature market and revive a struggling product all at the same time. In looking at why its Alba hot cocoa mix was doing so poorly against rivals Carnation and Swiss Miss, the Heinz marketing team noticed that Alba's ingredients were different. Alba contained more calcium—a fortunate coincidence because medical publications were just then reporting on the disease osteoporosis, said to be caused by a lack of calcium. Result: a product name change to Alba High Calcium. Ads show a young, attractive woman exercising as the text explains that women forty-five and over need calcium to keep their bones strong. Sales are now 50 percent higher than expected.

SEARS. While Sears managed the past during the 1970s and 1980s in many areas, its Mature Outlook program was a glowing exception. Started in the mid-eighties by

Allstate Insurance, a Sears subsidiary, Mature Outlook is a consumer-oriented benefits organization open to shoppers age fifty and older. For $9.95 a year, seniors receive a $100 merchandise coupon at Sears, a special Holiday Inn discount coupon, subscriptions to a magazine and newsletter, and other benefits. So far, Mature Outlook has drawn a membership of about 1.4 million, says Sears official Otto Georgi. "We feel this is Sears' marketing channel for the fifty-plus market, which everybody has identified as the growing segment of our population," says Georgi. "We feel comfortable with the program and are confident we have obtained successes from it."

PROVIDENTIAL HOME INCOME PLAN. Sometimes when you ask the question, What do seniors want from us? the answer will be: special products. Since many seniors have much of their net worth tied up in their homes, future-focused financial institutions have begun to offer "reverse mortgages." These products allow the customer to cash in on some of their equity while living in their home until they die.

Providential Home Income Plan offers reverse-mortgage loans in six states. Participants receive a monthly payment based on a price calculated by the company. When the owner dies or moves, the home is sold and the loan repaid. The product is new but the market is vast, according to the first-year experience of Providential. Launched in 1989 with projections of $25 million in closed loans for its first year, the company ended up writing $100 million in reverse mortgages.

The demographics are solidly behind additional growth. Some 13 million Americans aged sixty-five and older own their homes free and clear, and according to Providential's own estimates, all that unencumbered real estate amounts to $750 million to $1 billion. Although "house rich," a large number of older Americans are living at or below the poverty level.

What do seniors want? Not new products, necessarily. "Seniors buy for the experience a product can give them, not for the joy of owning more things," observes gerontologist Ken Dychtwald, founder of Age Wave, Inc., a research and consulting firm. Dychtwald believes seniors want experience, life satisfaction and meaning. After a lifetime of spending, most people, even middle- and low-income seniors, feel they have the things they want.

"Simply addressing conscious wants and needs is not sufficient," observes Charles Schewe, professor of marketing at the University of Massachusetts in Amherst. "With older segments an added dimension, 'life satisfaction' provides a unique opportunity for differentiation. Life satisfaction reflects one's ability to take pleasure in everyday activities, to consider life meaningful, to hold an optimistic outlook, to feel successful in achieving goals and to hold a positive sense of one's self."

Making Bucks from Baby Boomers

The mature market has paid big dividends to companies that sought it out and tried to understand it. The baby boom can also bring rewards . . . or penalties if you fail to change along with it.

The best way to cash in is to pay close attention to boomer preferences and respond accordingly. This is the essence of changing with your market. Here are some examples, starting with a famous magazine that didn't stay in touch with its boomer readers:

PLAYBOY MAGAZINE. *Playboy* was the victim of a demographic shift. Aging baby boomers, new sources of information and entertainment as well as the growing availability of alternative sources of soft pornography through cable-television, video and competing magazines, combined to dim the magazine's appeal. *Playboy* was once a leading source of information about cars, stereos and clothes for its target readership of college-educated men in their twenties and thirties. These days, the reader's choices have expanded. Hundreds of special-interest publications satisfy the informational needs *Playboy* once filled. "Any subject we write about is likely to have a whole magazine [about it] now," says Bill Page, a *Playboy* spokesman. *Playboy*'s circulation had dropped from its peak of 7 million in the mid-seventies to about 3.7 million by early 1990.

THE LIMITED EXPRESS. The Limited Express chain adroitly recast itself by observing how its prime customers were maturing. The clothing stores once targeted postadolescent girls; today they cater to contemporary women with sophisticated tastes.

If the process of recasting sounds easy, it isn't. Even some of the best marketers have missed shifts in the baby boom market. Consider the following example of a company that belatedly changed a previously successful strategy.

CLUB MED. While Club Med's clientele was busy getting married, settling down and having kids, the international club operator didn't adjust to keep up. The company continued to position itself as a place for good-time singles by featuring ads full of young, beautiful people. Club Med paid for this oversight with flat sales for several years, despite building new resorts and pumping in $370 million to renovate old ones. The French-owned company owns 117 vacation "villages" in twenty-six countries. After years of impressive growth, the firm peaked in 1986 at 220,000 guests entertained;

two years later 218,000 spent vacations there. Meanwhile the company was facing increasing bypass competition from cruise lines and others.

Finally the company launched a new advertising campaign designed to ride the age waves in a more profitable direction. Although the beautiful people weren't gone from the ads, they were joined by more diverse people. The new television spots focused on all the things vacationers could do at a Club Med resort. In one, a fiftyish couple relax by a waterfall, play golf and take a stroll on the beach. In another, a chubby club-goer in his forties munches on lobster, cake and other fattening foods.

Club Med has taken other steps to ride the age wave and to prove it's no longer just a refuge for sun-baked singles. Some resorts now feature Mini Clubs—child-care facilities with trained supervisors, children's play equipment and planned activities. To further boost this segment, the company has established certain months when children can stay free with their parents and has sponsored family-oriented activities.

Creatively Coping with the Baby Bust

The first two age waves represent new customers and new opportunities. The third wave, the baby bust, threatens to restrict your source of employees. That's because busters—those born between 1965 and 1978—are in short supply.

As a result, the United States is headed for a severe labor shortage over the next decade—a shortage that could affect your profitability and ability to compete. The labor supply will grow slowly in the 1990s—less than half as fast as it did in the seventies. And by the year 2000 we will experience a sharp decline in those aged twenty to twenty-nine, from 32 percent of the population to 21 percent. The number of young workers entering the job market will shrink by as much as 10 percent in the next decade. The decrease of women and young workers entering the work force and increased efforts to stem the flow of illegal immigration will lead to these lower growth rates.

What can you do about these negative trends? The usual tactic is to raise wages. Then, when higher wages don't work, the tendency is to intensify recruiting. But in the 1990s, these tactics may not succeed. What may work is a combination of tactics and lots of innovative thinking.

Let's look at some businesses that are already dealing with this change, that have chosen to manage the future instead of the past. As you will see, they are finding ways to: 1) improve the productivity of existing workers, 2) attract and retain workers in creative ways, and 3) automate operations. Future-oriented managers increasingly realize that winning in the 1990s involves all three.

SLEEP INNS. At the Sleep Inns motel chain, the labor shortage is being taken into account in the design of each facility. For example:

- Instead of having the night manager idle during much of his shift, Sleep Inns are designed so that the laundry room is just behind the front desk, allowing the person to man the desk and also prepare tomorrow's sheets and towels.
- The washer-dryers are user-friendly. All the night managers have to do is load and unload the machines and push a few buttons. Once they instruct the washer that a load of white sheets has been inserted, the washer's onboard computer automatically draws the right amount of bleach and detergent and adjusts its cycle time accordingly.

- To eliminate the need for the front desk to handle keys, guests use their own credit cards to unlock their doors. Other advantages: the front-desk computer can automatically turn off the heat or air-conditioning when a guest checks out of a room, saving energy.
- Nightstands are bolted to the wall so maids don't have to vacuum around the legs. The shower stall is round, eliminating corners and cracks that collect dirt.
- The security system helps the manager track a maid's time to the minute. To enter a room, the maid inserts a card that tells the front-desk computer where she is. The computer can later provide a productivity printout.
- Even the extensive use of shrubbery and foliage has a labor-saving purpose: there are fewer lawns to mow.

Companies like Sleep Inns are only beginning to scratch the surface. Labor-saving design features will bring competitive advantage in the future by eliminating the need for as many workers. For example, most businesses can achieve marked gains simply by taking a look at how accessible they are. Are the forms customers fill out and the signs they read easy to understand and follow without help? Or do customers regularly have to ask your employees for assistance? Customers don't enjoy having to ask any more than your people like being interrupted. Yet, most managers never consider how customers access their business.

STOP & SHOP. Design features can help businesses significantly reduce their labor requirement. So can a user-friendly technology. At many Stop & Shop superstores in the New England area, customers can use touch-sensitive computers to help them find what they're looking for. To find the chicken soup, press C and watch a directory of all items beginning with C appear on the screen. Touch the screen again for the item you want and a map of the store appears with a flashing trail directing you to the right aisle.

The computers are a big help in Stop & Shop's gigantic superstores, which are between 60,000 and 67,000 square feet—nearly three times the size of the company's regular supermarkets. First used in 1986 in the chain's Medford, Massachusetts, superstore, the computers have been installed in thirty-six of the 117 Stop & Shops. "Everybody is using them," says a company spokesman. "We have total acceptance in all age groups."

PIZZA HUT. Instead of operating the business for the sole convenience of management, future-managing firms try to find out what the people who work for them really want. Often, doing this has less to do with money than with eliminating unpopular rules and policies.

Since 1987, Pizza Hut has paid increasing attention to the issue of employee turnover. The Wichita, Kansas–based company began managing the future when it conducted focus groups that produced new ideas about what the chain could do to curb turnover. The answers came back loud and clear: Get rid of those demeaning brown polyester uniforms. Pizza Hut crews now wear snappy slacks, Polo-type pullover shirts and caps styled for the 1990s.

Pizza Hut has also adopted other strategies aimed at employee retention. It has introduced Sharepower, a stock ownership program spawned by Pizza Hut's parent company, PepsiCo. "Sharepower brings the opportunity to own stock in the company, previously available only to senior management, all the way down to employees who may be washing dishes," says a company spokesperson.

Pizza Hut has also been a pioneer in tapping the nation's handicapped population as a labor source. The company has launched a pilot program called Jobs Plus, designed to train and employ the disabled. Partially funded by the government and the Social Security Administration, the program places disabled persons with personal "job coaches" in Pizza Hut restaurants where they are trained in tasks ranging from folding pizza boxes to cleaning tables.

ORIGINAL RESEARCH CORPORATION. One company that has distinguished itself with a creative approach to the baby bust is Chicago-based Original Research Corporation, or ORC II for short. Founded in 1987 by Howard Tullman as a spin-off of an insurance appraisal business, ORC II offers a new type of service—follow-up calls to customers for auto dealers and other service companies. What Tullman knew he needed was increasingly difficult to come by in the Chicago area—part-time, motivated, detail-oriented phone operators who were good with people and who would work for low pay.

Sound like a tall order? You bet. But by building the company from the beginning with employee needs in mind, Tullman managed to tame the labor shortage and turn it into the company's competitive advantage.

After some experimentation, the fledgling firm found that applicants from employment agencies didn't work out. As Tullman says, "They had had a lot of jobs and didn't have the proper level of concern." His solution was to begin recruiting college students who were, although less experienced, open-minded and eager to master the work.

In the battle for employees, offering flexible hours is expected. Many employers in tight labor markets offer this incentive. ORC II went much further.

Students need flexibility. So instead of offering, say, a choice of shifts, the company allows employees to set their own hours, which they can change every two weeks. They can work more hours during the semester and then cut back for exams or vacations. They can start at almost any hour of the workday. And if they need to work less than the minimum fifteen hours per week—or skip work altogether for a while—the company tries to accommodate them.

Scheduling would seem to be a nightmare given such a lenient attitude by management. And ORC II's managers are the first to admit that it requires attention to keep the operation running smoothly. To eliminate under-staffing, the company hires and trains more than enough callers. Then it makes the job so interesting that students yearn to work there. It does this through:

- *Self-development programs.* Employees are encouraged to learn about topics that have little to do with work but that boost morale. Two or three times a month, callers are relieved of their duties for thirty-to forty-five-minute coaching sessions on topics ranging from handling confrontations to listening skills. In addition, they get time off (up to three hours a month) to pursue in-house courses that aid their development: how to use a calculator, balance a checkbook, write a concise memo—skills they aren't likely to learn on campus.
- *Creative perks and bonuses.* Part-timers can qualify for job upgrades and quarterly raises. Students who exhibit exceptional commitment are allowed to work full-time during the summer and vacations.

Good attendance is rewarded with coupons good for such things as sweatshirts, gym bags and free long-distance calls.

- *Participation in decision-making.* Relatively few people work full-time at ORC II. But even part-timers are given a voice in rules, such as dress codes and bonus plans. The company invites employee suggestions.
- *Training.* Nearly half of the students who start the company's four-week training program don't finish. Either they can't do the work the way it has to be done or they lack the commitment. After employees are trained, their work is monitored regularly. For many students, this is the first on-the-job training they've received, and they are appreciative because it helps them develop positive work habits.

Because ORC II makes such efforts to recruit and retain high-caliber employees, the company doesn't have to worry about a labor shortage. Instead, the quality of its work force is its competitive weapon.

As the age waves sweep through our economy they can pull you under or they can carry you to higher profits. The secret is to anticipate and respond to these inevitable trends.

Whatever the age of your customers, you'll find it essential to cater to their need for alternatives and customizing. Why? How? Turn to the next chapter to learn about the fourth Driving Force: Choice.

CHOICE

*Exploiting the "Have It Your Way"
Imperative*

The worst thing in our business is being out of stock.
—Import/export
Entrepreneur

"IN RUSSIA," OBSERVES a recent immigrant, "you stand in line for half an hour to buy beer. Then you have one choice. Here in America, you go into the supermarket and you walk down these gleaming aisles, totally in awe of the selection. There are dark and light beers, foreign beers, lite beers, even beers with no alcohol! You end up spending thirty minutes deciding which one to buy. In the end, you lose about the same amount of time . . . but the American way is a lot more fun."

Fun for the customer, maybe, but not for the business leader. Offering more choices—whether of beers, fabrics, insurance policies or money market funds—puts greater demands on you and your organization. It requires greater product knowledge on the part of your associates, more skilled coordination, more technology—in short, more complexity. That complexity makes it hard to maintain the mind-set that the Driving Force of choice spells "opportunity" rather than "pain in the neck."

But easy or not, offering customers the right new choices is destined to be one of the top challenges of the nineties. This chapter discusses how to make the Choice

Imperative work *for* you rather than *against* you. It ends with the eight key principles necessary to exploit the Choice Imperative. But first, let's look at what's driving this force of change and how it has splintered the marketplace.

HOW AND WHY CHOICE IS CHANGING OUR LIVES

The eighties heralded an explosion of choices for American consumers. Every television commercial, direct mail brochure, subway sign and newspaper ad conditioned consumers to want greater choices. So many alternatives have been thrust at them that the proliferation can be, not liberating, but tedious:

- The simple act of buying sneakers affords 1,000 styles to pick from.
- At AJS Warehouse in Atlanta, the owners add about 1,500 pairs of shoes per week to the store's inventory of 15,000 Italian and Spanish shoes.
- The IBM PC has over 30,000 different software programs.
- Car buyers can choose from 572 makes and models.
- The typical credit-card holder receives more than three catalogs per day from September through mid-December.
- Toothpaste now comes in 138 different varieties—tubes, dispensers, decorator colors, toothpaste for smokers, for folks with sensitive teeth, for coffee and tea drinkers, for those with yellow teeth.

And on it goes.

For the business leader, the choice explosion presents entirely new challenges. In a choice-driven society, brand loyalty is diminished as consumers experiment with new ones. Loyalty must be continuously reinforced.

What's pushing this push for choice? One factor is increased competition. Deregulation, for instance, brought on choices consumers never had to make before: long-distance carriers, phone manufacturers, cable companies. Technology is making a difference, too. Because of more flexible equipment, manufacturers can make more permutations to a product, can extend their lines ad nauseam, far beyond what most distributors and retailers can handle.

Racing toward Overchoice

"The society of the future," Alvin Toffler wrote in his 1970 book *Future Shock,* "will offer not a restricted, standardized flow of goods, but the greatest variety of *unstandardized* goods and services any society has ever seen. We are . . . racing toward 'overchoice'—the point at which the advantages of diversity and individualization are cancelled by the complexity of the buyer's decision-making process."

Toffler's future has come to pass. Bombarded with information, the consumer is forced to become a mini-expert in thousands of categories. With any given purchase, the explosion of choices involved can easily cancel out the equally strong desire for speed and convenience. Choosing isn't as much fun as it used to be.

Not long ago, *Los Angeles Times* essayist Beth Ann Krier wondered (only partly tongue in cheek) whether *choosing* a headache remedy might be a new source of headaches. "Even if you've figured out the differences between aspirin, acetaminophen and ibuprofen," she wrote, "and you know whether you want regular or extra-strength formulas, with or without sinus, arthritis

or antacid medication thrown in, you then face the cap-
sules, tablets or caplets decision. Oh, and don't forget
those coating options. Among the latest: 'gelatin-coated,'
'enteric-coated,' 'safety-coated' and 'Toleraid micro-coat-
ing.'"

Indeed, the freedom to choose from dozens of painkill-
ers or 450 models of videocassette recorders is offset by
the tyranny of *having* to choose. Consumers' fear that
they may make the wrong choice causes anxiety, even
buying paralysis. Should I wait until this product goes on
sale? Can I find it cheaper elsewhere? Will my friends tell
me I've blown it if I buy this model? How much research
and price comparison is enough? Will the new version
make this one obsolete? Such questions haunt buyers.
"We hear over and over again that people have trouble
making choices about buying decisions," observes David
Pittle, technical director of *Consumer Reports* magazine.

How the Marketplace Has Splintered

How has the push for choice affected the marketplace?
Increasingly, markets are "demassifying," splintering
into submarkets and specialized niches. Consumer tastes
are no longer homogenized by the mass media. Indeed,
the media itself reflect the trend toward diversity. CBS,
NBC and ABC continue to lose viewers to cable, video-
cassettes and independent channels. The push is inexora-
bly toward unique goods and services that consumers
have a hand in designing themselves—sofas, cars, benefit
plans, etc. Expanding choice is also a by-product of an
increasingly affluent and diverse society. Consumers cele-
brate their ethnic heritages and socioeconomic stations in
life. Rather than a melting pot, America has become a
salad bowl of unique individuals, races, creeds, lifestyles
and age groups.

Market segmentation is nothing new. In the auto industry, Henry Ford's refusal to offer consumers different models and colors hurt the company for years. His pronouncement that customers could have "any color so long as it is black" became notorious as the wrong way to respond to changing times. It was GM's legendary (and innovative) chairman Alfred P. Sloan, Jr., who first conceived the idea of a "car for every purse and purpose." The trend ever since has been toward more makes, more models, more options, more colors. The ultimate example is GM's new Saturn car. Customers will have an unprecedented hand in customizing each car, which will then be assembled by robots.

What *is* new is the degree of segmentation. Today, there are nineteen distinct subcategories for autos, and another eleven for trucks and vans. GM's Pontiac division offers a Gran Prix with a turbocharged V-6 engine, even though demand for such an engine is minimal—perhaps as few as 4,000 cars. Why would GM tool up to fill such a small demand? Because the company doesn't want to miss any niche. One percent of the entire $190 billion auto industry is more than a company the size of Polaroid ($1.86 billion).

The Choice Imperative pervades every industry. Choice has become a key source of competitive advantage for countless businesses. Federal Express offered customers a new choice—next-day delivery. Mo Siegel, the Colorado entrepreneur who founded Celestial Seasonings Herb Tea, expanded the customers' choice. He gave them a lifestyle alternative to the traditional caffeinated black tea. Mrs. Fields Cookies offered customers a new choice—convenient store-bought cookies that were as good as or better than homemade. And Toys "Я" Us exploited the Choice Imperative (as well as Driving Force 6: Discounting) to gain control of roughly 40 percent of the U.S. toy market. The company has thrived because, as founder Charles Lazarus is fond of saying, when parents have no clear idea of what to buy, they go to the store with the biggest selection. That's the power of the Choice Imperative.

Choice can even give you the power to attack an entrenched market leader. McDonald's key competitive advantage has always been its fast, assembly-line system. Over the years the company offered a greater selection. But the one choice they couldn't offer was "have it your way." Customizing each burger would have thrown a monkey wrench into McDonald's system, which requires standardized orders to work. Thus, Burger King gained competitive advantage by marketing choice. You, the customer, could ask them to hold the ketchup, grill the onions or whatever your heart desired. By astutely using the power of choice, Burger King made considerable inroads into McDonald's lead.

HOW TO EXPLOIT THE CHOICE IMPERATIVE

American society won't be going back to the one-size-fits-all mass markets. Customers will gravitate to businesses that offer them more styles, colors, options and price levels.

So where's the payoff? How can your organization derive competitive advantage from the choice explosion?

The Choice Imperative presents critical questions every day. Should you add this option, feature, color or package? What are the consequences? Such questions all too often are made piecemeal, on the basis of outdated assumptions rather than as part of an overall strategy. How do you build that strategy? Below, I've identified nine key principles future-oriented businesses are using to meet the choice challenge.

Principle #1: Audit Your Customers' Moments of Truth

Mastering the challenge of choice begins with identifying each moment of truth, those all-important points of customer contact where customers have a choice during the purchasing cycle. Then ask which alternatives the customer really values, and which ones you can eliminate because they really don't matter to the customer. Keep customer satisfaction clearly in focus.

Mastering the Choice Imperative means understanding your customers better than anybody else. It means figuring out how you can deliver more of the options, features and packages that customers value most, while skipping the ones they really don't care about. And it means avoiding the no-win game of adding options just because the competition has done so. The challenge is to discover meaningful choices that differentiate your company from the competition.

Principle #2: Define Ultimate Choice

Earlier in this book, we spoke of the importance of speed in fulfilling the customer's request. With the Choice Imperative, the corollary is one-of-a-kind manufactured-on-the-spot products and services. In many service businesses, the "product" is indeed manufactured to order. The hostess begins "manufacturing" your dining experience the moment she asks whether you'd prefer smoking or non, in a booth or at a table.

Try this exercise in envisioning the ultimate choice. Imagine you own a clothing store. What if, instead of being measured by a clerk, a customer could stand in a laser measuring machine about the size of a metal detector in an airport. This done, the clerk helps the customer select colors, fabrics and styles. After selection, the order is transmitted to a manufacturing facility where work begins immediately. The next day, by overnight express, a custom suit arrives ready to wear.

Of course, this scenario is just a farfetched exercise in imagination, right? Wrong. It's being done already.

Often the future arrives sooner than we expect. We are living in a time when we must be open to the farfetched and far-out. Not to be trendy, but to find ways to add value for customers.

So let yourself dream. No restrictions. What is the *ultimate* in choice and customer satisfaction for your business? Take a moment right now to visualize what that might mean. Whatever the ultimate and no matter how unachievable, the goal must be to chip away at those things that impede its realization. The innovative business is the one that discovers how to do the impossible. That's what managing the future is all about.

Principle #3: Be Willing to Customize

Everybody knows that the days of "one size fits all" are over. Yet the extent to which businesses are willing to accommodate each individual customer varies greatly.

Customizing, which is to say meeting each customer's request even if it's not what you normally do, is one of the most powerful things you can do to build a lasting customer relationship. Look at it this way: How many times have you, as a consumer, made a request of a business only to be told, "We don't offer that." What did you do? You probably continued looking around until you discovered a firm that could meet your request.

What happens when new or unusual requests are made of your company? Certainly you won't be able to accommodate all of them, but at least try to meet as many as you can. Make it part of your mission to be the business that is willing to customize, willing to meet those off-the-wall requests.

I once heard of a restaurant that would make anything the customer requested, even if it wasn't on the regular menu. So long as the chef had the ingredients, the rule was, "It may take a little longer, but we can do it." Broadcasting this attitude and publicizing the way you are ready and willing to accommodate unusual requests sends an important message to your associates that they're to be open-minded to customers about such possibilities. Such an attitude engenders innovative thinking, which is what managing the future is all about. Every market starts with those "unusual" requests.

Federal Express was born because Fred Smith kept getting requests from businesspeople who needed to charter one of his aircraft to get a package to another city in a hurry. The Packaging Store was born because existing freight forwarders didn't want to be bothered with oddball shipments like rocking chairs. And on it goes. Be the business that figures out a way to fill those special requests, even if you have to charge extra. *And certainly make it a point to keep tabs on the requests you're turning over to your competition.*

Principle #4: Know Your Limits

I've just advised you to customize your products and services to the specification of your customers. Now I'm going to suggest that you balance your flexibility with a healthy understanding of your limitations.

Trying to do everything and be everything can turn

into a no-win game, unless you add choices strategically. Some grocery stores, for example, are on a never-ending treadmill of adding products requested by customers. Is the solution to double the size of stores every so often? But then store size becomes a problem for customers who find large stores inconvenient. The grocery business has limits. So does yours.

1. *Space is a limit.* The recent trend by supermarkets toward requiring manufacturers to pay for shelf space is but one example of the limitation on choice. Manufacturers can extend their lines all they want, but they must pay to introduce and house them on grocers' shelves. This trend has accelerated the disappearance of slow-moving products and increased the barriers to entry. It has made it especially difficult for smaller, less-established companies to compete. Is this same trend headed for your industry?

2. *The need to maintain quality is a limit.* I lunched recently with a colleague at a midpriced chain restaurant in Ventura, California. As we looked over the menu, we noted it had the largest selection either of us had seen. We could order from the extensive breakfast menu, or from a huge selection of lunch salads and entrees. Yet when our selections came, my soup of the day was bland and the Reuben sandwich was improperly cooked. My friend had the same reaction to his meal. The array of choices left no favorable impression; the poor quality made a lasting negative impression. Simply adding mediocre choices, then, is not the way to gain competitive advantage. In some industries, it may be better to have a limited, high-quality selection rather than a wide selection that pleases no one.

3. *Complexity is a limit.* Computers and automated systems can help mitigate complexity. But your salespeople, managers and other employees must still be able to inte-

grate those choices. The typical IBM representative now has more than 2,000 product and service offerings to keep up with. Each rep knows less and less about more and more. At the precise time when customers need in-depth information to make intelligent decisions, IBM's frontline representatives have become less helpful.

4. *Lack of meaningful differences is a limit.* Over 200 breakfast cereals now have bran in them. Most of them are hardly distinguishable to the palette. Only their marketing and advertising set them apart.

You must find a way around these and other limitations before exploiting the Choice Imperative negatively impacts your attempts to take advantage of other Driving Forces. For example, Wal-Mart recently decided not to build any additional hypermarkets because, even though their huge size gave customers a huge selection to choose from, the customer wanting just a few things was severely inconvenienced by having to search those items out. Result: fewer visits and lost sales. By recognizing your limits, you are in a better position to keep your quality up as well. Better to do fewer things well than many things poorly.

Principle #5: Ask the Customer (and ask some more)

Before you introduce a new choice, ask customers what they think. That sounds like simpleminded advice, yet often the customer is the last to be consulted.

"In today's marketplace," observes futurist Laurel Cutler, "you're crazy to interpose anything between you and the consumers. If you want to know what they think, you go, you ask the questions, you watch the faces, you watch the body language, you decide whether the people are just being polite and want to say yes because they are in a rush to finish their errands. This is the undelegatable part of giving birth to any new product."

A lot of excitement was generated during the 1980s with the all-suite hotel. The lodging industry readied a revolution—but the customer got lost in the euphoria. Hoping to lure traveling executives, the all-suites promised a "home away from home": VCRs, microwaves, even a popcorn maker in some cases. And two rooms instead of one, perfect for women business travelers who might want to have a meeting in their rooms. What they didn't have, unfortunately, were the services customers valued: full-scale restaurants, bellhops and twenty-four-hour room service. Many business travelers weren't in their rooms long enough to care about the extra space. One survey revealed that fewer than one in ten business travelers prefer all-suite hotels. All-suite hotels may not be the wave of the future after all.

Offering the wrong choice isn't hard to do. For instance, what do car renters want most? When customers were polled, the answer came back loud and clear: They wanted frequent-flier miles. They cared little about such frills as cellular phones, computerized directions and power windows. Yet one rental car giant responded by phasing out frequent-flier programs and adding cellular phones and computerized directions and power windows.

The suite-builders and auto-rental companies failed to listen. How can you avoid the same mistake? Ask your customers. And keep asking them until you're sure. And then keep asking and checking in. Probe the customers' thinking in an open-ended way. For example, if you ask what colors customers prefer among current offerings, you won't get ideas for new colors. Instead of asking about existing products, find out what features and choices the customer would propose instead.

Principle #6: Hang Out with Customers

Businesses begin to manage the past the moment they stop listening to customers.

Debbi Fields, the founder and president of Mrs. Fields Cookies, once described to me why she visits stores and gives out free cookies. It's her favorite way of finding out what's on customers' minds. While she pores over every letter from customers, she also heads out to the front lines on a regular basis. "I spend my time seeing what customers see and working the counters so I can really relate to what customers look at in terms of image. When I listen to them I know how they want the cookies packaged, I know what they are looking for in terms of flavors. On top of that, because I'm a busy consumer, I also think in terms of my own needs. If you literally become a consumer, then you find out what's available and you can evaluate what your own needs are and what you like and don't like. The ideas you get are incredible."

I am convinced that hanging out with customers is one of the secrets future-managing leaders share. Alfred P. Sloan, Jr., who took a small company named General Motors in the twenties and built it into one of the world's largest corporations, was no exception. At least once every quarter he made it a point to travel to a distant city, introduce himself to the local Chevy dealer, and ask the dealer's permission to work as a salesman for a couple of days. Before he returned to Detroit he'd do the same thing at two other dealerships, sometimes selling, sometimes working as an assistant service manager. Then he'd return to headquarters full of new ideas and insights about changes he wanted to implement based on his observations of changing customer behavior and preferences, market trends and style trends.

Not that his intuitions were GM's only source of customer feedback—far from it. Even as early as the 1930s, GM had the most up-to-date and comprehensive customer research department in American industry. And yet, according to the head of customer research at the automaker at the time, by actually working with customers on the front lines, Sloan spotted more trends and more important trends than did customer research, and he spotted them earlier.

Principle #7: Remember that Nobody "Owns" the Choice Advantage

For years, Baskin-Robbins was the largest ice cream franchise in America, in part because it offered customers the widest selection. It seemed to "own" the choice advantage. The "31 flavors" slogan became a symbol of our choice-driven society. Who would ever come out with more?

Baskin-Robbins began to believe that it had a lock on the ice cream market. If you wanted variety, you went to Baskin-Robbins. Then, along came Häagen-Dazs, which attacked Baskin-Robbins on the premium side. And just down the street, what's this—frozen yogurt? Why didn't Baskin-Robbins install frozen yogurt machines? Actually, they did, almost ten years after the fact, and only after there was a frozen yogurt shop on every corner, and Americans were hooked on premium ice creams. Baskin-Robbins got slammed because they believed they owned the Choice Imperative. And at that point, their customers, many of them baby boomers increasingly concerned with counting calories but not wanting to give up sweets, bypassed Baskin-Robbins for a frozen concoction they believed was healthier.

In what ways does your company now dominate the

choice advantage? How do you guard against believing that you own the choice advantage with your customers?

Principle #8: Innovate Constantly

Many business leaders now believe that choice is *always* a no-win game. Their philosophy is, "Let's wait and see what the other guy does. If it works, we can always copy it."

This is not only a false assumption, it is shortsighted. Yes, the pioneer takes risks in being first. But he also gains valuable lead time and experience. The difference comes down to whether the choice is truly an advantage or just an easily copied gimmick.

Merrill Lynch's Cash Management Account (CMA) provides an example. The idea, hatched during a brainstorming session by Merrill's Tom Chrystie and several Stanford researchers, was to create an all-purpose brokerage account that would include a checkbook, a credit card, a money market fund, a margin account and other frills. It was quite a battle to get the idea through the bureaucracy. But Chrystie, then the firm's chief financial officer, lined up Ohio's Banc One to provide a Visa card. Gradually he put all the pieces in place.

At the time Merrill introduced the account, no other brokerage firm in America had dared to offer such a service. Almost immediately, bankers challenged the legality of a brokerage firm offering such an account. The resulting publicity discouraged Merrill's rivals from coming up with a matching plan. Several states banned the CMA, and even Merrill's own brokers were cool to it. Merrill Lynch Chairman Donald Regan, a supporter of the idea, had to save it from a slew of skeptics. At first, anyway. Because it offered customers variety and choice, it took off. By 1982, when other brokerage firms began offering similar accounts, Merrill Lynch was already well positioned. It had sold half a million CMAs, with assets of $32 billion. By 1989, the company had sold 1.3 million with assets of $155 billion. The nearest brokerage rival had sold only 170,000.

Obviously, Merrill Lynch obtained competitive advantage by giving consumers choices in the way they managed their money. Merrill benefited by being first, being able to fine-tune its product and carve out an identity for the product while other brokerage firms waited to see if it was safe.

The easier they are to replicate, the faster your choice advantages may become table stakes in a zero-sum game. If they're unique and the customer perceives them as offering a distinct advantage, you're probably onto something.

Principle #9: If You've Got It, Sell It

As department stores have floundered in recent years, they have forgotten their advantage: selection. A specialty shop typically has only a limited selection. A department store can house two to three times more items. If selection and choice are part of your competitive advantage, sell that. Rather than seeing its size as being an advantage, the typical department store understaffs the sales floor. Customers feel overwhelmed rather than transported. With wide choice, it seems, comes the need for knowledgeable salespeople to help the customer navigate. (I'll have more to say about this in discussing Driving Force 8: Customer Service.)

Today's changing, fragmented marketplace is definitely more complex. But this same complexity confronts your competitors. Who's going to survive and thrive? Those who view the Choice Imperative as a chance to attack. The winners will create new options and alternatives that add meaning to the customer's experience and value to the product. Your company can be one of those winners if it follows the nine principles outlined above.

What else do winners need to navigate the nineties? One requirement is an understanding of changing lifestyles and how they can make or break a business. We'll explore this Driving Force in the next chapter.

LIFESTYLE

Benefiting from Changes in the Way We Live

Retailers did well for the past twenty years almost without paying attention to market changes. Now they have to.
— KURT BARNARD
Publisher, *Retail Marketing Report*

Rubbermaid is the best argument I've ever seen that American business can be competitive.
— JOSEPH KOZLOFF
Research Vice President, PaineWebber

I don't believe that the average patron wants to sit down and enjoy a meal as much. They want to eat and get going; there are too many other things to do.
— ORRIS ABBOTT
Restaurant broker

COMPANIES THAT DON'T take the time to understand and respond to lifestyle changes often end up in the red. Just ask Singer Sewing Machine Company.

In the early seventies, Singer made the best-known sewing machines in the world and dominated the global market. But in the late 1970s, sales began to decline. According to a former executive of the company, the first year this happened, management attributed the decreasing sales to bad weather. The next year, they assumed that the oil crisis was the culprit. When sales sagged for a third year, they blamed cheap foreign machines.

Finally, the company convened a special task force. Only then did Singer realize that its chief product was the victim of a lifestyle change: women entering the work force in record numbers.

This new lifestyle changed women's priorities. They had less time to sew. They had less *interest* in sewing. Singer's real competition were other leisure pursuits that were more in keeping with the new career-oriented lifestyles. Add to that a flood of cheap ready-to-wear clothing from southeast Asian factories and the cost savings of sewing-your-own began to disappear.

Singer was devastated by a lifestyle change. This is not to imply that Singer's executives were incompetent. They simply weren't prepared. In a world where change is accelerating, Singer's experience serves as a warning to large and small businesses alike. Lifestyle shifts can spell boom or doom to a business. In this chapter we'll define lifestyle and examine how several companies have coped with this powerful Driving Force. Then we'll discuss specific strategies to improve your batting average when the market throws a lifestyle change your way.

WHAT IS A LIFESTYLE CHANGE?

Lifestyle changes can occur in any arena of customers' lives and involve work, leisure, child-rearing, marital status, safety, environmental concerns and so on. The bottom line is how and where and why those customers spend their money.

"You steer the ship by trying to catch the tides" is the conventional wisdom regarding lifestyle changes. But day-to-day business isn't that simple. How do you distinguish a long-term tide that can float you safely into harbor from a short-lived wave that can push you into the shoals?

The trick is to know the difference between *fads* and *trends*. Fads—wine coolers or leisure suits or suntanning salons—create short-term demand. Long-term trends meet real consumer needs having to do with how we live today.

Fads	Trends
aerobics	fitness
"Baby on Board" signs	increased safety consciousness
wine coolers	decreasing alcohol consumption
oat bran mania	health consciousness

Many people believe that trends emerge randomly, without rhyme or reason. "Why try to predict the unpredictable?" they say. But trends can often be detected, like problems in a car. One morning your car takes longer to start than usual, but you ignore this as a fluke. The following day a puff of black smoke appears when you start up, but you're so busy you ignore it. The next day the car stalls in the middle of freeway traffic. You're stuck.

Trends are like this, too. They *can* be detected if you're perceptive, open-minded, alert and responsive. They can be understood and used to improve business decisions. Let's see how several well-known companies have gotten lifestyle changes on their side.

LIFESTYLE CHANGES IN THE MARKETPLACE

You gain competitive advantage by responding to a lifestyle change in a way that makes you different from your competitors. Being the first to do something for your customer is one way to create this uniqueness. On the other hand, if you wait until everyone else responds to the change, you've gained nothing. If everyone in your industry is doing the same thing, you're not responding, you're reacting. Nothing ventured, nothing gained.

American industry is learning this lesson. But sometimes it comes the hard way, at the expense of millions of dollars and market share. To see how this Driving Force is shaping the nineties, let's follow a single lifestyle change—the growth of women in the work force—and see how it affected three different industries.

Rubbermaid—Riding the Lifestyle Wave

The best example of a company that is *pro*active rather than *re*active is Rubbermaid, the Wooster, Ohio, maker of everything from toys to spatulas to plastic lawn chairs. Rubbermaid has profited from numerous lifestyle changes in American society better than perhaps any other U.S. company. That's the assessment of more than 8,000 senior executives, outside directors and financial analysts who regularly name Rubbermaid one of the ten most admired companies in the United States.

Much of the credit goes to Stanley Gault, who became chairman of Rubbermaid in 1980. Since then, Rubbermaid has increased sales fivefold and profits sixfold. Gault reorganized the lackluster organization into semiautonomous companies and tied compensation to performance. He also decreed that 30 percent of sales must come from products less than five years old. With stiff competition (some 150 companies make housewares and nearly all undercut Rubbermaid's prices), growth might seem difficult to come by. But not at Rubbermaid. One reason: The company's leaders are adept at searching out new ways to grow. Rubbermaid makes it a priority to stay on top of changes in customer lifestyles. It uses these insights to change existing products, or add new ones.

Gault freely acknowledges the role of sussing out and meeting the needs of changing lifestyles in Rubbermaid's impressive growth. What's the company's philosophy when it is considering entering a new market?

"Our main thrust with new product development," says Gault, "is to look for categories that have not been served before or that we feel can be served better by what we are proposing. With the Servin' Saver line, for example, the original objective was to design a line of food keepers that would recognize the consumer's need to see what's inside, as well as to conserve space, which we kept hearing was a major concern. The Tupperware product—a very fine, quality product, by the way—followed a conical shape. Our design allowed two or three items in the same amount of refrigerator space."

Much of Rubbermaid's closeness to its customers comes from frequent focus groups. It was from these focus groups that the company observed—of all things— an attitudinal shift about leftovers.

"With the rise in the number of working women," Gault explains, "and with increasing numbers of single-parent and single-person households, more people were preparing food in advance, sort of having 'planned-overs.' In addition, with the increased emphasis on health, consumers are buying more fresh vegetables and more expensive prepared foods. So the category was healthy, and Tupperware pretty much had it to themselves, with about 80 percent of the market."

How to attack Tupperware where it was most vulnerable? Not by an appeal to consumers based on Rubbermaid's higher quality. More than anything, the name Tupperware stands for a quality product—the seals on its containers are so tight that they do not leak even when submerged in water. Then where? Why, with Tupperware's distribution method, wherein customers have to attend a party, place orders and wait for the order to come in. Did the fact that 50 percent of women were working outside the home make less appealing the idea of spending an evening at a party centered around buying plastic storage containers?

"Sure it was," Gault acknowledges. "We heard in our focus groups women saying, 'I haven't got time to go to a party.' The last thing they wanted to do was go to some party that they only said they would go to three weeks ago because they couldn't turn down their neighbor or sister or friend from the office. The convenience of being able to get the product at a supermarket whenever they shopped, at a very attractive price, was important. So those three things, product, lifestyle and distribution, were areas we improved upon by listening to the customer and asking ourselves, 'How can we do this better?' "

At Rubbermaid, asking how a product or method of distribution can be improved is part of the philosophy that drives the organization toward the future. In seeking out and capitalizing on such vulnerabilities as Tupperware's lifestyle-dated distribution system, Rubbermaid has compiled an enviable batting average.

Their secret? "We don't have any secret," Gault insists. "We are constantly on the prowl to observe how things are being done today, why they are being done that way, what could we do to do it better, in particular using plastic as the material." Yet whereas so many companies get blindsided by lifestyle shifts, Rubbermaid uses them to great advantage. Rubbermaid's version of *kaizen,* the Japanese word for constant improvement, is intermingled with some serious trend watching.

"We are *voracious* readers," Gault adds. "We read articles on lifestyle and demographic issues constantly. And we are all very involved in all of our businesses. We do make excellent use of the demographic information that is available. By pursuing this, we have a propensity to be able to recognize and identify products or feature opportunities that respond to the perceived needs of the customer—whether it's a retail customer or an industrial, commercial or institutional customer."

Lifestyles and the Direct-Selling Industry

Avon, Tupperware, Amway and other direct-selling companies all took a beating as a result of the lifestyle change of women entering the work force. Between 1980 and 1986, their U.S. sales were flat, rising slightly toward the end of the decade. It was then and only then that they discovered they needed to adapt to this important change—by going to the workplace. If the direct-selling industry was to prosper, it had to grasp the significance of the Lifestyle Imperative and respond.

When women began the exodus from the home and into the workplace in the early 1970s, Avon did nothing. The beauty products company waited a full decade before changing its distribution rules. Restricted to specific territories, Avon's sales force sold mostly door-to-door. But with more women in the workplace, there were fewer potential customers at home when Avon came calling. The company also had problems retaining its sales representatives, losing them to the workplace as well.

In 1985, troubled by declining profits, Avon loosened its restrictions. Although some sales territories do exist—and are functioning well in rural areas—most Avon representatives cross over traditional boundaries to take advantage of what the company finally identified as its main target: sales in the workplace. Roughly a third of Avon's earnings now come from such sales. This shift, as well as rapidly increasing overseas sales, helped Avon improve its sales from $2 billion in 1985 to more than $3 billion in 1989.

Even Tupperware, the company that pioneered the suburban purchasing party in the early 1950s, is responding to the Lifestyle Imperative. Not by going to conventional retail sales, but by recognizing that women have moved out of the home and into the workplace. Traditional in-home Tupperware parties still account for three-quarters of the company's business. But alternatives such as the office party, the stop'n'shop party and the rush-hour party have moved Tupperware's products out of the home and into the workplace, where they are exposed not only to America's working women but also to working men.

The rush-hour party, for office workers at the end of the workday, seems like a more workable solution to the needs of nineties lifestyles: Customers are able to buy quickly and leave, the employer doesn't feel cheated by the downtime, and the Tupperware sales reps are happy because they can report higher overall sales per attendee than at in-home parties.

As both Avon and Tupperware's experiences indicate, exploiting the opportunities that changing lifestyles present can mean altering one's distribution methods to what works best for the customer, not what works best for the seller.

The Apparel Industry

Women entering the work force. We've already seen how this lifestyle change impacted Rubbermaid, Avon and Tupperware. It has affected the fashion industry as well. The unprecedented numbers of women entering the work force in the mid-1970s needed new types of attire. In 1976, a little-known fashion designer named Elizabeth Claiborne Ortenberg and her husband, Arthur Ortenberg, decided to go after that emerging market. Claiborne did not look at the demographics and projections of social forecasters; instead, she used her own conversations with other working women to research this lifestyle change. "I listened to the customer," says Claiborne. "I went on the selling floor as a saleswoman, went into the fitting room, heard what they liked and didn't like. Not that you do exactly what they want. What you do is digest the information and then give them what you think they ought to have."

Claiborne was one of the first designers to encourage the change from the navy-blue suit and bow tie "uniform" to more expressive, feminine attire. She came to believe that as women became more secure in business, they would desire clothing that expressed this increased confidence. She also took a hard look at the shape of the typical American woman and designed for pear-shaped bodies instead of forcing women into fashions that looked good only on anorexic fashion models.

The result: Liz Claiborne, Inc., was the most profitable of all publicly held firms during the 1980s, according to *Forbes* magazine, averaging 51.8 percent return on equity. Claiborne clothes and colognes ring up annual sales of over $400 a square foot, twice the department store average. LCI is consistently the number one or number two vendor at department stores.

But not even Liz Claiborne, Inc., is immune from the impact of changing lifestyles on the fortunes of businesses that get out of touch for even a moment. In the spring of 1988, the company bet heavily on the return of the thigh-high miniskirt. It bombed.

Because of the incredible rate of change today, managing the future means listening and listening some more. The apparel industry was slow to realize that its customers were getting older and that changing lifestyle patterns meant that today's working woman would not leap at the latest fashion fad.

If there's anyone who needs to keep on top of changing lifestyle trends, it's Leslie Wexner, chairman of The Limited, based in Columbus, Ohio. How he does it is instructive. Wexner travels constantly, spending as much as 60 percent of his time on the road—in New York, Paris, Tokyo or anyplace else that will help him spot trends and keep his imagination stimulated. One buyer for the company who traveled with Wexner comments, "We'd go to Europe five times a year and to the Far East just as often. Les would have a list of stores he'd want to see, and we'd just walk and talk constantly, sometimes two cities a day."

In Paris, Wexner pulled out his wallet and bought flowers from a vendor whose display caught his fancy. The vendor had tacked flowers to the side of his booth, rather than simply laying them on a table like the others. Wexner realized it was the excitement in the display that had made him want to buy. Back in Columbus, he ordered new displays in all his stores—displays that echoed the ideas he'd brought back from Paris. The new look featured sweaters and blouses cascading down walls, with mirrors and chrome everywhere to dazzle.

HOW TO PROFIT FROM LIFESTYLE CHANGES

Leslie Wexner's antennae are up all the time, looking for ideas, for trends, for lifestyle changes. You, too, must put up your antennae if you hope to benefit from the Driving

Force of the Lifestyle Imperative. You must learn to scan the future and turn changes into profits.

Scanning the Future

As the speed of change accelerates, a haphazard approach to change detection is no longer enough. Everyone is trying to anticipate what will come next. To prevail you must devise a *superior* method, a way to discern more clearly and more quickly what is coming.

You don't have to be perfect at doing this, just better than your competition. Consider the story of two hikers in the woods. One says, "I smell a bear!" and immediately puts on his jogging shoes. The other one snickers and says, "Jogging shoes! You can't outrun a bear!" The first hiker replies with a smile, "I don't have to outrun the bear—I just have to outrun you."

The point of the story is this: You can't hope to spot every trend. But by establishing an early warning system, you'll at least spot most of them ahead of the competition. The better informed you are, the fewer unpleasant surprises you'll receive. And that's a key: Defenders are always reacting. But attackers are opportunity spotters and innovators. They shape events to their own advantage. Reacting or shaping—what mode is your organization in right now?

Leaders of companies that have been blindsided by a change will admit that they "should have seen it coming." Often they had no established way to diagnose the meaning of events and changes in their markets. Even companies with elaborate forecasting departments often don't hold them in high regard. Yet this function lies at the heart of guiding an organization toward the future it wants, rather than a future that happens by default.

In my many interviews with America's leading innovators, I've observed how serious they are about figuring out the future. Today's business leaders need a scanning system to alert them to threats and opportunities. Such a system forces your perspective beyond the day-to-day. It helps you to focus on how well your company is changing with change. Studies have shown that business executives, as a group, are uninformed about the social environment. One survey of a thousand top and midlevel managers revealed that the majority see the world as a huge jigsaw puzzle. Their spheres of understanding are limited to small pieces of that puzzle. They have little idea about what is going on in any of the other spheres. And here's the important point: It's what's happening in those other pieces of the puzzle that can wipe you out or enable you to create profitable new possibilities.

Setting Up a Future Scan System

How can you find out more about the other pieces of the puzzle? The secret lies in learning to use four components of a future scan system.

COMPONENT #1: ADJUST YOUR READING HABITS

Take stock: What newspapers, magazines, newsletters and trade publications do you read? Stop now and make a list. Then ask yourself: Is this the reading diet of a future-focused executive? Am I getting trivia, noise and clutter, or am I learning about other pieces of the larger puzzle?

I've met and interviewed many great opportunity spotters. They are all bullish on the written word, and they make their reading time count. Here are nine techniques you can put to use right away to get more from your reading.

1. *Read for surprises.* Look for what's different, incongruous, new, worrisome, exciting. Professional social forecasters call this scanning and monitoring. They scan to monitor trends. The goal is to notice trends before the media does. If you can do that, you know your early warning system is working effectively. But if you're reading about developments in your field in *Reader's Digest,* you know you're behind—and that means you're vulnerable. So read for what jumps out at you. When you spot something unusual, ask yourself: How can this trend become an opportunity?

2. *Read broadly.* Many executives feel they barely have time to flip through the newsweeklies, much less general-interest publications. Be forewarned, lack of broad information can hurt you. My recommendation is that the business leader subscribe to at least a dozen magazines and newspapers, even if you don't read them all as they come in. Save them. When you're taking a flight or have a block of free time, whittle away at the stack. Even if you only skim them, you'll pick up a wealth of information and you'll notice connections and start seeing patterns of change emerge.

3. *Read for different points of view.* One executive I know told me he reads everything from *The Wall Street Journal* to matchbook covers for the variety of inputs. Accept the free literature you're offered, send off for those sample issues of new publications and constantly reinvigorate your reading materials. You never know where a new idea may come from.

Buckminster Fuller, the great inventor, supposedly always bought the top right-hand magazine when he visited a newsstand, no matter what magazine it was. Once his purchase turned out to be a nature magazine carrying an article about the structure of the eye of a housefly. Fuller read that article, thought about the fly's eye, and came up with a nifty little invention he called the geodesic dome.

4. *Read for the wheat and skip the chaff.* There's plenty that you can safely skip. Celebrity profiles, crime reports, the latest scandal—these stories won't help you spot opportunities. Spend your time reading feature stories, where you'll often find the most valuable information.

For example, features are on the far right and far left columns of *The Wall Street Journal* and other major newspapers. Your local paper may not carry feature stories on current issues and trends. If not, you must rely on magazines or subscribe to a national newspaper. Also, if your local newspaper is short on wheat and long on chaff, be sure you subscribe to one of the newsweeklies, such as *Time, Newsweek, US News & World Report* or *Insight.*

5. *Read up on at least one new subject every week.* It might be a new technological or scientific breakthrough, or an emerging political or social issue. Make it a point to read a long in-depth article on the subject, even if you aren't particularly interested. You may be wondering what this has to do with opportunity spotting. Remember, the more you know and understand about the other pieces of the puzzle, the less likely something will blindside you.

6. *Read the local newspapers when you travel.* You'll find amazing tidbits plus local insights and viewpoints. You can also compare business climates and spot new opportunities in regional markets.

7. *Subscribe to newsletters and trend reports.* Some are very expensive—the *Yankelovich Monitor* runs $15,000 a year. But if you keep your eyes open, you'll discover excellent trend letters for your industry. By subscribing, you earn the right to call the editor on occasion to check out your hunches or to bounce around ideas. Two of my current

favorites are Roger Selbert's *FutureScan* and Michael Kami's *Strategic Assumptions.* In addition, some local banks publish trend reports and are happy to put you on their mailing lists. These reports are like vitamin supplements for your regular information diet.

8. *Read the nonfiction bestsellers.* Keep a list of titles gleaned from periodicals, newspapers and radio interviews. Keep your list active and you'll soon develop your own network of "book news."

9. *Read your mail.* Or more to the point, scan your mail, especially your junk mail, for patterns of change, for information on who's doing what and why. Look for what's different about the direct mail you're receiving this year as opposed to last. The mail, if you look at it as an opportunity spotter, becomes one more window on the world.

COMPONENT #2: CONNECT WITH PEOPLE

People are the second component of your future scan system—the people surrounding you, the people you depend on for ideas and insights. Are they opportunity spotters? Are they looking for the big picture, as you are? Do they spur you to think more deeply about current events, new inventions, the latest developments in your field? Or are they focused solely on daily details, organizational politics and immediate needs? The people in your life have a tremendous influence on how you think—perhaps more influence than you realize or care to admit.

Evaluate your current circle of contacts. If they can't help you keep abreast, take action immediately. Join networking groups and professional associations. Attend conventions and trade shows. Take along your business card. When you meet people whose ideas interest you, establish contact. Send them a note when you get back to the office, and cement the contact with a follow-up phone call.

The time you spend with others can widen your base of information if you learn to ask the right questions. Make people the cornerstone of your early warning system.

COMPONENT #3: OBSERVE YOURSELF

The third part of your system is self-observation. The greatest opportunity spotters are self-observant. They listen to their intuition. Intuition plays a crucial role in spotting trends. But you must be sensitive to the signals. You must be willing to respond when your internal early warning system sends notice that something important is happening.

Self-observation also helps by letting you "see the world as if you are the whole market." You look at your own needs, likes and dislikes, and apply them to your business. Imagine yourself as a customer of your own company. Then ask, What would I want that isn't presently available? What do I like? What turns me off? By asking yourself such questions, you stay tuned in to customers. Ask the questions often enough, and you'll begin to anticipate what customers will want next.

COMPONENT #4: CHALLENGE YOUR ASSUMPTIONS

Chances are, you're a specialist in some field. That specialty is your comfort zone. Staying in that comfort zone can be dangerous to you, your career and your organization. Markets and customers are changing faster every day. Some of the biggest assumptions we make turn out to have major flaws. A good friend of mine brought this point home after his Dallas-based real estate investment syndicate was forced into bankruptcy after the tax law changes of 1986. "We all began to think the bonanza days would go on forever, despite the tremendous over-building of office complexes," he told me. "And then the balloon burst." What does "everybody know" to be true in *your* industry? It could turn out to be a house of cards.

For example, everybody knows that Americans are eating out more, right? That's a lifestyle change every-body agrees on. The restaurant industry today is over-built because in the 1980s lots of people said, "People are eating out more, cooking less. Let's open a restaurant and make a killing." Nearly 40,000 food establishments opened their doors between 1985 and 1987, according to Dun & Bradstreet. Now, in many American cities, restaurants are retrenching, not expanding. There are simply too many of them. One recent report, focusing on the Southern California market, warned of a shakeout, citing, among other factors:

- customers turned off by high prices, long waits and indifferent service—negative factors that came with the 1980s' restaurant boom
- bypass competition from area supermarkets which have added deli counters, salad bars and gourmet prepared foods
- too many food choices (overchoice)
- lack of time or interest in spending the time it takes to receive the value of the dining experience
- baby boom couples staying at home more because they have babies

Unfortunately, what "everybody knows" can become a false assumption. Once everybody knows something about a lifestyle shift, it is probably too late to cash in on it. Instead, it's better to look out ahead a bit to see where the changes are taking us.

Turning Changes into Profits

We've discussed how to spot trends with a future scan system. But what do you do when you notice a lifestyle change? Discovering trends is only the first step in profiting from them. What you do with the insights you discover is what counts.

"Problems," observed the great industrialist Henry J. Kaiser, "are merely opportunities in work clothes." Creative solutions occur to those who are prepared to act. You may find they come to you in pieces, pieces that you must then bring together. Thus your idea evolves and improves as you get feedback and continue to work on it.

Want more inspiration? Here are six real-life companies that have managed the future in the way they turned lifestyle-related problems into profits:

Lifestyle problem: Sales of McCormick spices were flat. Working women and men prefer easy-to-prepare meals. They use fewer spices, unsure which spices belong with which foods.

Innovative response: McCormick repackaged its spices, phasing out the tin cans, introducing plastic jars and adding freshness seals. Plastic jars allow the occasional user to check for signs of deterioration. Small recipe cards with each bottle show inexpert cooks which spices to use on which dishes.

Lifestyle problem: Non-smoking Americans are concerned about passive cigarette smoke, especially in enclosed spaces such as airplanes.

Innovative response: Northwest Airlines went one step further than the federal government, which in April

1988 banned smoking on flights of two hours or less. On the same date, Northwest introduced Fly Smoke-Free, banning smoking on all its North American flights. "It generated a ton of favorable reaction. . . . It was really a pioneering move," says Bob Gibbons, a spokesman for the airline.

It was also a business decision, says Gibbons. "We did some research and found that 70 percent of our frequent flyers supported smoke-free flights broader than the federal rules. We even found that 20 percent of the smokers favored a smoke-free policy. We lost some customers but we gained more than we lost." Since then, of course, smoking has been banned on all domestic U.S. flights.

Lifestyle problem: While Americans are eating more prepared foods than ever before, no restaurant chain has managed to serve the customer's multiple needs of speed, convenience and wholesomeness.

Innovative response: Soup Exchange, a cafeteria-style restaurant chain based in San Diego now offers the convenience of self-service, the wholesomeness of all-natural foods and the atmosphere of a medium-priced family restaurant.

Lifestyle problem: Termites must be eradicated from homes, offices and other structures. Homes have to be tented, allergic reactions can occur and pets and plants can be harmed. Result: Customers are increasingly concerned about harmful side effects.

Innovative response: Tallon Termite & Pest Control, based in Long Beach, California, has come up with a two-pronged method to eradicate termites without toxic chemicals. Tallon's Blizzard System uses chilled liquid nitrogen to freeze termites in inaccessible areas. A second technique—the use of electric-powered heat strips on infested wood—was introduced in mid-1989. Both tactics were developed by son Joe, Jr., the firm's vice president and director of research and development. Yet another son, Jay Tallon, serves as chief executive officer.

Since 1985, the privately held company's revenues have increased nearly tenfold and plans are in the works to expand the technology from its base in central and Southern California to franchises in other Sunbelt states.

Lifestyle opportunity: Americans are living longer. The fifty-year-old man today will live to age seventy-six and the average fifty-year-old woman can expect to live to age eighty-one.

Innovative response: Coastal Colony Corporation of Manheim, Pennsylvania, manufactures factory-built cottages designed to house an elderly relative who wants to maintain independence while staying near the family. The prefabricated structures can be set up in the backyard of the typical suburban home. If the family moves, they can take the cottage with them.

The cottages range from a 288-square-foot efficiency unit that costs about $17,000 including set-up, to a three-bedroom, two-bath 1,000-square-foot home that can be built, shipped and installed for about $37,000. The cottages have senior-style features: wider doorways, lower counters and lever door handles rather than knobs for easier access.

Lifestyle problem: Smog in Los Angeles is deplorable. It is produced in disproportionate amounts by pre-1975 cars and trucks that still burn leaded fuel. Environmental groups have urged air-control agencies to implement alternative fuels, such as methanol, which would be costly for gasoline companies.

Innovative response: Atlantic Richfield Company (ARCO) spent $20 million to research and develop EC-1, a new fuel designed specifically for pre-1975 vehicles. EC-1 is the first effort to demonstrate that gasoline can lead to cleaner air as well as alternative fuels. The company spent an additional $10 million to advertise its product and received tons of positive free publicity in the process.

Lifestyle changes. To capitalize on this Driving Force, you must build a future scan system. And when you spot a new trend, you must be prepared to act with new products and new services. How should you price those products and services? That's not an easy question in the nineties. To find the right answer for your company, turn to the next chapter, where we examine the Driving Force of discounting and the perils of price competition.

DISCOUNTING

Positioning Your Business in an Era of Price Competition

The way we got started was because other people left an opening for us. If we sit on our duffs, they're going to do the same thing to us.

— SOL PRICE
Founder, Price Club

Help-U-Sell is to the real estate industry what the printing press was to book publishing.

— EARL NIGHTINGALE
Author of *The Strangest Secret*

DISCOUNTING IS ONE Driving Force that every business must understand to prosper in the nineties. *Every* business. In the next decade, discounting will spread to virtually all industries, including the professions. Skeptical? Consider these examples:

- In the second half of the 1980s, discounters overtook department stores in unit sales of apparel.
- For the first time in its 116-year history, Anheuser-Busch has cut beer prices across the board, even for market leader Budweiser.
- Taco Bell permanently dropped taco prices from 79 cents to 49 or 59 cents. Customer traffic jumped 30 percent in 1989.
- Jenny Craig Weight Loss Centers slashed sign-up

prices from $400 to $185. Per store volume shot
from $40,000 per month to $100,000.
- Sears shut down its stores for two days in 1989 in
order to change the price tags on thousands of
items.

Once the unstoppable juggernaut of American retailing, Sears could not resist the discounting wave. Your
business could fall prey, too, unless you are prepared. In
this chapter, we'll see why discounting is such an over-
powering trend, how it has already transformed the
marketplace and where it is headed. We'll finish by discussing two very different ways to reposition your company to meet the challenge.

WHY DISCOUNTING IS A DRIVING FORCE

We all know what discounting means—selling goods and
services at less than retail. This simple idea has evolved
into a deep-seated trend that is transforming every American industry. It may be the most powerful, most dangerous Driving Force of all.

Why dangerous? Because discounting as practiced in
the nineties will bring more than lower prices. It will
inevitably change the rules of entire industries, creating
new winners and new losers in its wake. Once an industry
is revolutionized by the discounting wave, it is never the
same. Customers are changed by seeing value in a new
way. Manufacturers are changed because they again must
deal directly with retailers rather than with middlemen.
Traditional retailers are changed because they must
quickly offer additional value and service.

As an industry develops, it adds more and more inter-
mediaries until the structure becomes inefficient, and

121

therefore vulnerable to the discounter. Across the board the U.S. economy is reacting to a condition of inefficiency from too many layers between the maker of a product and its end users with higher markups for the consumer. Each layer—each distributor, wholesaler or other intermediary—adds costs. Discounters change the rules by taking an industry back to a more primitive stage, where the goods flow directly from the manufacturer to the retailer.

Two recent entrants:

MEDCHOICE. Based in Fullerton, California, Med-Choice serves the medical practitioners' need for low-cost supplies and equipment, from lab coats and latex gloves to dental bonding systems and tongue depressors. The general public is expected to account for a third of sales, even though many items will be off limits to those without a medical license. Founder Ted Morgan, also a founder of Office Club, started MedChoice because the medical supply market was dominated by small vendors. Distribution by the small family-owned businesses meant profit margins as high as 40 percent for distributors, compared to margins of 10 percent to 15 percent for discounters.

AUTO GIANT. Based in Long Beach, California, Auto Giant will hawk auto parts and accessories at 50 percent to 75 percent below suggested retail. The auto parts market, which traditionally enjoyed healthy markups, was ripe for a discounting revolution. Auto Giant plans 30,000 square feet of retail space in each store, plus 15,000 square feet for service bays.

Any way you slice it, discounters like MedChoice and Auto Giant are highly sophisticated players. Their strategies are well thought out and well executed. They are powerful attackers.

Discounters are among the most powerful forces in the marketplace today. When a discounter moves into a market, it comes in the guise of the consumer's ally and the traditional company's enemy. It screams from rooftops that consumers have been taken for a ride, that they have been fleeced by high prices.

Crown Books brought discounting to the book retailing business. President Robert M. Haft has a standard line: "Books cost too much, so I started Crown Books." He finishes with, "So remember . . . if you paid full price, you didn't buy it at Crown Books." The residual effect in consumers' minds is that if you paid full price for *anything,* you were ripped off.

In fact, Crown Books is a perfect example of the Discounting Imperative. Opening its first store in Rockville, Maryland, in 1977, the company had grown to over 260 stores by 1990. Crown's formula has been to operate relatively small, self-service stores in neighborhood shopping centers rather than in higher-rent regional malls. In exchange the customer gets discounts of up to 40 percent on hardcover bestsellers. At first publishers were skeptical of the approach, and of the chain's then 24-year-old founder. "Not only didn't the publishers think we would make it," Haft told *The New York Times*, "they used to look at me funny, and one of them always called me 'young man.'"

The New Price-Sensitive Consumer

The assault by the discounters has led to a new, cost-conscious consumer, a consumer in rebellion against perceived price gouging, a consumer in rebellion against perceived manipulation of value.

The consumer who will predominate in the 1990s is better informed and more sophisticated about how and where goods and services can be acquired at the lowest possible price. Part of this new sensitivity to cost has come about because the consumer's standard of living often has not kept pace with rising tastes and aspirations. Indeed, we frequently see statistics like these:

- Between 1973 and 1983, average family income of Americans in the twenty-five-to-thirty-four age group plummeted 17 percent, according to Census Bureau figures, even though there were often two wage earners instead of only one in a family.
- Only 30 percent of U.S. households have disposable income.
- Median income of unmarried men aged twenty-five to thirty-four nosedived 26 percent between 1973 and 1983.
- Forty-five percent of single mothers with children live below the poverty line.

What statistics like these seem to indicate is simply this: Large numbers of Americans are quietly strapped and are looking for bargains. They are likely to be lured by discounters. Discounters today have the attention of more than just K Mart shoppers.

Many of these new price-sensitive consumers are the 76 million baby boomers who are now in their peak earning and acquiring years. Having run into the nightmares of overextended credit cards, they have been chastened. Not that they have stopped wanting; quite the contrary. But having come the hard way to the timeless verities, in the 1990s they will demand value. And regardless of their economic station, additional expenses will take a toll on disposable income. Dollars once designated for traveling or entertaining now go toward such things as taxes, college tuition, health and auto insurance and child care. Baby boom consumers have begun to realize that their tastes and aspirations cannot be achieved without savvy spending. Thus, the new price-sensitive consumer may shop at Nordstrom in the morning, but at Price Club or even a flea market in the afternoon.

Do It Yourself: The Ultimate Bypass Competition

The new cost-conscious consumer is one force behind the discounting phenomenon. Also at work is the rise of the do-it-yourself customer. When prices get so high that many people can no longer afford a product or service, the do-it-yourself innovators and those businesses which help to accommodate them come to the fore.

Seventy-five percent of all U.S. households now engage in some form of do-it-yourself home improvement, up from 40 percent in the 1970s. Retail sales of home improvement products have been growing about 10 percent a year, reaching $82 billion in 1989. In the past decade, handyman homeowners overtook professionals as buyers of building supply materials. These days, they cart off nearly 60 percent of such goods, and even when they don't do the work themselves, an increasing number of consumers are becoming buy-it-yourselfers, saving the markup that contractors often charge on materials.

Moreover, doing it yourself and cutting out the usual jobbers is the rage in arenas far from the hammer and paintbrush crowd. Consider how advances in computing and desktop publishing equipment are changing the printing profession. A San Francisco photographer relocating to New York needed new business stationery in a hurry. On the afternoon before his departure, he sat down at his personal computer and laser printer to produce a professional-looking letterhead and business card—in three hours.

Not long ago, this project would have required a type-setter, a pasteup artist and a print shop. All three businesses have been bypassed by virtue of new technology.

Indeed, the growing self-publishing movement has taken hold precisely because many knowledgeable merchants prefer to do it themselves, from printing to sales to distribution, in exchange for a much higher percentage of the profits. And with sales of instructional materials booming—books and audiotapes and seminars that teach people how to do everything from multilevel marketing to motivating frontline employees, the do-it-yourself movement will continue to expand.

About the only arena this trend won't affect is medicine, at least not to the point of do-it-yourself surgery. Still, as the price of conventional medical treatment continues to skyrocket, a self-care movement has already emerged. Consumers can now check for everything from herpes to pregnancy via home-testing kits without consulting a doctor. Home care, a less-expensive alternative to hospitalization, is a $14 billion business and growing.

Discounting and the Other Driving Forces

In a moment, we'll look further at discounting's inexorable march through the American marketplace and what this may mean to your business. But first, it will benefit us to spend a paragraph or two exploring how discounting interacts with the other Driving Forces.

Early on in this book, we saw how Sears got into trouble when it stopped managing the future and became complacent about its position in the marketplace. Now we are in a position to see why: Sears was attacked by retailers who exploited two Driving Forces to which it had no correspondingly powerful counterattack: discounting and choice (mall competitors began offering trendier goods in brighter surroundings). Discounting attackers often *combine* discounting with other tactics that emerge directly out of their superior understanding and positioning regarding the ten Driving Forces of change. To wit:

- Toys "Я" Us, a discounter of children's toys, also provides customers with greater choices and a unique "techno-edge" that we'll learn more about in Driving Force 9. Result: Toys "Я" Us controls over a quarter of the $16 billion toy industry.
- Soft Warehouse, a growing chain of computer superstores, similarly relies on discounting and choice in its attack on traditional retailers. Its stores, in Dallas, Houston, Atlanta and Los Angeles, are self-service but do have salesclerks to answer questions and in-house repair operations and technical support staffs. Their prices are anywhere from 30 percent to 80 percent below retail.
- Circuit City superstores, which we'll learn more about in an upcoming chapter, also combines discounting with choice, convenience, speed and customer service to create a powerful force in retailing of major appliances and home electronics.

So as we discuss examples of future-managing firms, it's important to keep in mind that some successful attackers exploit other Driving Forces besides discounting to come up with their winning formula. Conversely, other future-managing firms use their understanding of Driving Forces which we have yet to cover, namely customer service, value-adding and quality, to *counteract* their opponents' discounting advantage. How else to explain the phenomenal success of Nordstrom department stores in an era of the price-conscious consumer, or Mrs. Fields

Cookies, which charges more than a dollar for a single cookie. But more about the strategies of these decided nondiscounters in chapters to come. For now, let's continue with our discussion of discounting.

DISCOUNTING IN THE MARKETPLACE

Discounting is such a pervasive economic force that examples are available from almost any field. I've chosen to focus on one manufacturing industry (cigarettes), one retailing industry (office products) and one service industry (real estate). They demonstrate the power of the Discounting Imperative. After considering these examples, we can turn our attention to the future of discounting. I'll let you listen in on conversations with two of America's discount pioneers, Sol Price and George Orban. Their insights show where discounting is headed in the next decade.

The Tobacco Industry

In early 1989, the Liggett Group, smallest of the six big U.S. tobacco companies, introduced Pyramid, a low-cost cigarette selling for 70 to 90 cents a pack. Liggett eschewed the usual rollout advertising, yet Pyramid was one of the hottest-selling new brands in years.

Liggett's experience underlines how discounting can jolt a staid industry—in this case, the $35 billion tobacco trade. For decades, cigarette prices were controlled by unspoken agreements among the six dominant tobacco companies. Faced with a dwindling market share, Liggett first broke ranks in 1984. It turned the industry on its ear when it packaged a quality cigarette in a nondescript black-and-white pack, slapped the name Flavor Lights across the front and priced them 35 percent below the competition. Liggett's pioneering generic cigarettes spawned imitators and then landmark litigation. Liggett sued Brown & Williamson Tobacco, another tobacco giant, charging them with predatory pricing practices and trademark infringement. A jury dismissed the trademark charge but ruled in favor of Liggett on the pricing issue and awarded the company $149 million in damages.

The tobacco industry's spats notwithstanding, the experiments of Liggett and others demonstrate the powerful allure of discounting. Plain-wrapped generic cigarettes have now been joined by branded generics, such as Liggett's Pyramid and RJR Nabisco's Doral labels. By 1990, cut-price cigarettes accounted for 20 percent of the market. The appeal of cheaper cigarettes is cause for concern in the tobacco industry, which worries that they may undercut demand for popular, highly profitable brands such as Marlboro and Winston. Discounting is yet another burden for an industry that has seen steadily rising taxes, flagging demand (from 625 billion cigarettes in 1982 to 525 billion in 1989) and mounting warnings about the detrimental health effects of smoking.

The Office Products Industry

Not long ago I was invited to address a series of regional conferences sponsored by the National Office Products Association. NOPA is the voice of small to medium-sized office products dealers and stationers.

As I researched my target audience in preparation for my speeches, I discovered an industry in turmoil. Practically overnight, the Driving Force of discounting was changing the way office products were distributed, at least in the retail sector. What initially started the revolution were the warehouse clubs; realizing the unusually high margins to be had, they began stocking more than just school supplies. Then, beginning in 1986, discounters with names such as Staples, Office Depot, Office Club and WORKplace opened some 300 superstores nationwide. Operating from huge warehouses, superstores were an immediate hit with customers and were a direct threat to traditional dealers.

Many small and midsized dealers had precious little time to realize what was going on, much less to respond creatively. Untold numbers went out of business, while across the board profit margins plummeted. NOPA's figures show that average net profits nosedived from 4 percent in 1978 to 1.9 percent in 1988. Hard hit initially were the mail-order discounters, such as Lincolnshire, Illinois–based Quill Corporation, the nation's largest.

"What we've learned is how ready people are to forgo service to get a good price at a superstore," notes Quill's president, Jack Miller. "It's amazing that someone will actually fight traffic, deal with parking, push a cart around and wait in line at the counter holding heavy items just to save $5. But it proves that price is an even more important marketing tool than I originally thought. We've been hearing a lot these days about how if you add value to a product, you'll be able to command a higher price. The real issue in this business now is, what can you do to charge less for your goods?" Quill was forced to slash prices even further.

Meanwhile, more superstores are on the way: 280 stores are planned by 1992. Will the smaller, independent dealers survive? In cities where superstores have congregated, such as Phoenix, dozens of dealers have disappeared in a few years' time. There are still a few independent grocery stores around, but not many; a few independent hardware stores around, but not many. At this point, the future of many midsized dealers has yet to be determined. Given the increasing number of home-based offices, the industry is growing. Many dealers may muddle through by taking a wait-and-see attitude. But those who hope to profit from change will identify and creatively exploit the Driving Forces they have going for them—notably their locational convenience, their value-added programs and their customer service. The clear choice dealers face is whether to passively allow events to happen to them, or take charge and proactively manage the future.

The Real Estate Industry

It's obvious how discounting can impact a product industry. And we've just seen the havoc discounting is causing in office products retailing. But the service sector is *not* immune either. Real estate is but one example of an industry that may be vulnerable to the Driving Force of discounting in the nineties. In 1981, 15 percent of home sellers sold their own homes. By 1987, 20 percent were going it alone.

According to the National Association of Realtors, the trend is expected to escalate in the 1990s. As it does, so will the number of businesses that cater to the discount yearnings of the do-it-yourselfers. The movement has already spawned newsletters, magazines and companies offering sell-it-yourself kits.

Why the change? For starters, increasing home prices have escalated commissions. Sellers see a chance to avoid the 6 to 7 percent fees of the traditional real estate brokers. Paying 6 percent made sense when homes sold for $50,000. But when homes sell for five times that much, the commission begins to eat up substantial equity. "The do-it-yourself movement is growing because nobody wants to pay $20,000 to sell a house they bought for $50,000 ten years ago," observes the publisher of one "for sale by owner" newsletter.

Don Taylor, a Mission Viejo, California, broker,

sensed the dissatisfaction on the part of home sellers and agents alike with the way homes are sold in America. In 1976, he founded Help-U-Sell. Instead of the traditional 6 percent, Help-U-Sell charges a set fee that averages less than half a typical commission. For this fee, Help-U-Sell counselors, who are all fully licensed real estate professionals, provide advice, access to the company's exclusive listing service, optional access to the Multiple Listing Service and guaranteed advertising in local newspapers. The home seller is offered a variety of choices, such as whether to host open houses and how much of the legwork involved in the transaction he or she will do, in exchange for a higher or lower fee.

Help-U-Sell was the first nationwide firm for do-it-yourselfers. Because Help-U-Sell and its ilk challenge the status quo, they are attackers. The traditional brokers become defenders.

How much will discounting impact the traditional industry? The answer seems to be that both discounting and the do-it-yourself alternative are inexorable and that the real estate industry cannot afford to be complacent. Indeed, in its 1989 annual survey of readers, *Consumer Reports* reported one of the lowest overall satisfaction rates ever with real estate agents. Nearly one-third of the readers who had used an agency in the previous four years reported trouble of one kind or another. The most frequent complaint: "The agent did not earn his/her commission."

What might traditional real estate brokers do to respond to the Discounting Imperative? They must increase their professionalism, police their ranks and add value by exploiting every one of the other Driving Forces. This means continuing to implement creative ideas that simplify the transaction for buyers and sellers alike. One example: video listings that allow prospective buyers to preview homes without driving around.

The Future of Discounting

We could continue with examples of how discounting is reshaping American industries. But we might be wiser to turn our attention to the future instead. Discounting is like a virus that is spreading to every industry it touches. And as it spreads, it changes. Two forces are central to these changes: the backlash phenomenon and the differentiation effect.

1. THE BACKLASH PHENOMENON

Discounters do not get a free ride. They face the backlash of the industries they attack. They will be met with every countermeasure short of actual warfare.

In challenging traditional retailers, Price Club founder Sol Price was well served by his training as an attorney. His first venture, FedMart, faced similar legal hurdles when it brought discounting to the retail industry. "Everything it did was examined by its competition, by legislative authority, by police authority, by manufacturers and by the Federal Trade Commission," writes Robert Drew-Bear in his book *Mass Merchandising: Revolution and Evolution.* "All of this was designed to 'catch' the organization so that it could be shown up to its members and to the public as something somehow sinister, or illegal or dishonest."

Sheralee Nyswonger has observed the backlash phenomenon firsthand. She had held numerous jobs in medical offices when the entrepreneurial bug bit. But instead of opening a beauty parlor or a dry cleaning store, she had the crazy idea to open a retail casket company—America's first.

"People are more price conscious these days," she told the *Los Angeles Times.* "If they know they can get something at Price Club, they'll go there and not to a department store." Her Hillmark Casket Gallery, in Loma Linda, California, sold caskets for 30 percent to 40 percent below funeral homes.

She thought she was getting into a nice quiet business but soon found out otherwise. Casket manufacturers traditionally sell directly to funeral homes, which cover their overhead costs by heavily marking up the price of the casket. The coffin markups are necessary, according to funeral directors, because service fees are not high enough to recover operating costs for such items as chapel and limousine use.

From her first day in business, Nyswonger experienced the wrath of the traditional funeral industry. That day, the owner of a local mortuary stormed into the shop demanding to know the identity of Hillmark's casket suppliers. From then on, the harassment did not stop. Because funeral homes are casket companies' major market, funeral directors wield a powerful influence over their suppliers. One casket manufacturer bowed to pressure from funeral directors and stopped supplying Hillmark. A trucking company refused to work with her. Then, as if on cue, the funeral directors in the east Los Angeles area began charging handling fees, at prices designed to wipe out the customers' savings. Hillmark Casket Gallery, while profitable from its second month in business, was forced to close in mid-1990. "We didn't close for a lack of customers," says Nyswonger, who has filed numerous complaints with the Federal Trade Commission.

Across the continent, two Marylanders also faced the heat of an entrenched industry. In 1985, Hugh Wilkinson and Dudley Briggs started the American Association of Cruise Passengers, a discount travel agency. An annual membership fee would include free trip-cancellation insurance and vacation financing. A high-volume business would make up for the discounts. "We were the first in, kind of like the McDonald's of the cruise business," Briggs notes. Whereas the average travel agent may book twenty cruises a year, he hoped to book thousands.

Customers loved the concept. The association sold 1,000 memberships in its first month. At first cruise lines and travel agents reacted positively, too. But suddenly they changed their minds and would no longer do business with the agency.

Discounters, though welcomed by consumers, are often vilified by the industry they attack. The firm that intends to use discounting as a strategy must be prepared to face the weight of the entrenched industry. Yet, to quote the great American philosopher Ralph Waldo Emerson, "Events are in the saddle and ride mankind." No matter how your firm is positioned regarding the Discounting Imperative, trying to stop it by putting discounting attackers out of business is a short-lived strategy at best. Discounting will come to every industry in time.

2. THE DIFFERENTIATION EFFECT

If the backlash phenomenon promises to affect the timing of discounting's arrival, the differentiation effect often brings even more profound changes. The differentiation effect simply says that if two or more strong players emerge in an industry, then they too, like the traditional firms in that industry, will be forced to differentiate, and price alone will no longer guarantee success.

For example, consider K Mart, the discounting pioneer. It was a leader in bringing discounting to the retail world in the 1950s, eventually expanding to 2,200 stores across the United States. But now there is a new kid on the block. The attacker is Wal-Mart stores of Bentonville, Arkansas. On the surface, the two discount chains have more similarities than differences. So why does Wal-Mart, with only 1,325 stores, have higher profits—$837 million versus $803 million for K Mart?

Wal-Mart has used differentiation to manage its future. It has aggressively defined differences with K Mart. As it grew, Wal-Mart copied many of K Mart's innovative ideas. Now, several independent surveys reveal that consumers associate K Mart with the past and Wal-Mart with the future. One study found that Wal-Mart shoppers rated the store significantly higher in esteem and spent more money than K Mart shoppers. Another study revealed that shoppers are consistently more satisfied with Wal-Mart.

How can this be? A visit to both stores reveals almost identical merchandise and similar prices. K Mart has poured millions of dollars into renovating its stores. Is it significant that Wal-Mart employees wear blue vests, while K Mart employees don't? Or that K Mart's logo, though highly recognizable, conveys the impression that the company hasn't changed since the 1960s? Or that Wal-Mart has wider aisles? Or that Wal-Mart has recessed fluorescent lighting while K Mart uses exposed fluorescent strips? Or that Wal-Mart clothing departments are carpeted in subdued tones, while K Mart uses cold, off-white tile?

Wal-Mart discounts, but also goes further. It has succeeded in setting itself apart as a discounter that tries harder to please the customer. The subtle difference was brought home to me while driving through the rural towns of my native South Carolina. As we pulled off the freeway we immediately passed a K Mart, then headed up the street to a Wal-Mart. No sooner had I gotten in the door than I was met by the "people greeter." This grandfatherly gentleman called out greetings as if he personally knew every shopper. When I asked a question, he answered with smiling hospitality. He knew where everything was, too. There was also a greeter back at the nearby K Mart, but she waited stoically until asked for information.

Such features signal to consumers that Wal-Mart is more upscale. The carpeting makes the apparel departments feel warmer and the padding underfoot makes tired shoppers linger longer. The subdued brown and white colors convey a warmer, less blatantly commercial invitation to shoppers.

Other discounters are also differentiating themselves not solely on the basis of amenities, but in other, less tangible areas as well. Until it saw the light, Newark, California–based Ross Stores, Inc., was just another discount apparel store. Not anymore. "Ten years ago shoppers spent two hours in an off-price store," says Alan Schlesinger, the company's marketing chief. "Today the average is forty minutes." Today, Ross Stores feature sparkling polished-glass display cases, gleaming chrome racks and name-brand designer labels. Ross installed brighter lighting. Borrowing an idea from department stores, it redesigned stores with clustered displays of matching outfits for time-constrained shoppers.

A Conversation with Sol Price

Where is discounting headed? Why not ask pioneer Sol Price, one of its leading proponents.

Before he started Price Club, Price was a crusading liberal attorney. In the 1950s, he founded the FedMart discount chain and built it into one of the nation's largest retailers. Along the way, Price has not only changed the rules, he's broken more than a few of them.

One of these rules is the Choice Imperative, which, as we saw in examining Driving Force 4: Choice, would seem to dictate that businesses carry as wide a selection as possible to meet a growing diversity of consumer tastes. Yet Price Club stocks a measly 3,500 items, compared to 80,000 at a typical K Mart. And Price Club outlets stock only one style of each, take it or leave it.

A second rule is the Convenience Imperative. Most retailers at least pay lip service to the Convenience Imperative. Offer your own store credit card. Locate near residential communities. Provide salespeople. Not Sol Price. He locates most of his stores in the middle of nowhere where land is cheap. He provides no store credit cards and doesn't accept anyone else's. He has no salespeople; customers must wander the spartan, dimly lit warehouses to search for what they need.

So what keeps customers coming back? Incredible bargains. Brand-name items are 40 percent less than at conventional retailers. Up to now, Price Club's guiding philosophy has been: *If the price is low enough, it's the only Driving Force you need to heed.*

"I always believed that there was too much money being spent on getting the goods from the manufacturer to the consumer," says Price. "Advertising, packaging and selection were artificially inflating the price. That's where I saw our opening, as a bridge between the manufacturer and the consumer." And Price again defied conventional wisdom with the type of customer he wanted to appeal to. Rather than go after the broad mass market, from the very beginning he sought to appeal to business owners who weren't big enough to qualify for the substantial volume discounts larger businesses received.

Over the years, the formula worked so well that Price Clubs have attracted a rash of imitators. Does he see the need to change the formula? Will he be forced to differentiate? "When you get other people doing the same thing you are," Price admits, "you have to differentiate.

Essentially, there isn't a lot of price differential between us and the clones. They come into our place and see what we're selling and they go to the same vendors and they put the same stuff out. So now everybody's trying to differentiate."

His counterstrategy is to go vertical. "We're manufacturing more of our own goods. We will go more and more to our own label. We think we've got enough credibility with our customers and enough volume now to be able to do that."

Price has other ideas for the 1990s, too, but is not keen on tipping his hand to the competition. Of one thing, though, he is sure—the need to keep innovating, experimenting, changing with change. "I've always believed," says Price, "that if you just sit on your backside and say 'if it ain't broke, don't fix it' that somebody's going to come along and fix it for you. What you did last year is ancient history. The way we got started was because other people left an opening for us. If we sit on our duffs, they're going to do the same thing to us. You've always got to be challenging what you're doing."

A Conversation with George Orban

If Sol Price is the father of discounting, George Orban is one of its leading promulgators. Orban is a Columbia MBA and former New York investment banker. Five different companies bear the Orban imprint in some way or another: Egghead Software, Ross Stores, Karen Austin Petites, Little Henry's Auto Service Centers and WORKplace.

Before he attacks a new industry with a discounting strategy, Orban looks for two things: distribution inefficiencies and changing technology. In looking at the software business in the early 1980s, he observed not only a rapidly growing industry, but one wherein, on the retail distribution side, at least, nobody was making any money. "And nobody was really performing a service to their customers," he recalls. "Stores were inefficient and unpleasant. The microcomputer software business combined the inefficiency in distribution and great technological evolution. It had both those critical elements." As a result, he was instrumental in growing the Egghead Software chain into a national concern.

Similar conditions made the office products industry ripe for discounting. In Miami on a business trip, Orban met an entrepreneur by the name of Harold Jaffe who ran two large office products stores in what had once been grocery stores.

"They were a mess," Orban recalls. "But when I visited those stores, I noticed a couple of things. One, Jaffe was doing a tremendous business in a lousy retail store. And two, as I started poking around I was astounded by the rate of growth in the office products industry and its consistent performance. The profit margins were high; everybody made money, even in recessionary periods. I made some mental notes about the industry and then in 1986, a fellow in Boston started Staples and I said to myself, if I don't get into it now, I never will."

In creating WORKplace, Orban made inventory control technology an integral part of the strategy. "It's now possible," observes Orban, "for a start-up company with relatively limited capital to put in sophisticated computer systems and communications systems so that they can deliver products to consumers much more efficiently than a guy like Sears who hasn't kept up. One of the reasons Wal-Mart and Ross Stores are so successful is because they've created more efficient vehicles for delivering products. At Ross, for example, we have a huge nonunionized distribution center, we have state-of-the-art computer systems and we can move product from the factory floor into the store in six days. Off-price retailers now amount to 10 to 15 percent of the apparel industry. Why? Not because anybody rode a wave of fashion; it was just a more efficient way of delivering product to the consumer. The department stores were locked into their traditional methods, and locked in with their old systems. If somebody had been courageous and said we are going to throw out the old way of doing things, they could have stayed with the times and protected their market share."

While Orban is a fervent believer that industries with inefficient distribution methods will continue to be vulnerable to discounting attackers, he also sees major strategic changes coming among post-discounted industries. Indeed, his WORKplace office and computer products superstores look more like The Sharper Image than Price Club outlets. "We sensed that as competition evolved everybody would do the simpler thing, which is to take a bare-bones, me-too approach," says Orban. "We chose to do something more difficult, but three years down the road, we'll be able to protect our market position better. We'll be able to establish a greater degree of customer loyalty. And in fact our stores generate a lot higher volume than anyone else in the industry."

HOW TO POSITION YOUR BUSINESS

So far in this chapter, we've looked at various businesses and industries from the standpoint of how discounting has impacted their bottom lines. Now it's time to turn our attention to your business and to examine how this deep-seated trend could affect your positioning strategy. The questions below, if you'll pause to consider each of them with pen and paper in hand, will assist you in discovering where you stand currently with regard to this Driving Force, and how to manage the future of your business.

Repositioning Yourself to Fight Discounting

1. How vulnerable are you to an attack by a discounter?
2. What might you do now to discourage such an attack?
3. How much price resistance is there on the part of your customers?
4. What is the likelihood that an across-the-board price cut, à la Taco Bell and Jenny Craig, would raise volume and thereby profitability?
5. How might you exploit the do-it-yourself trend? What services and products might you offer that would appeal to do-it-yourselfers?
6. How can you add convenience?
7. How can you add value?
8. How can you add lifestyle improvements?
9. How might you improve your customer service?

Repositioning Yourself as a Discounter

1. If you decide to position yourself as a discounter, what types of backlash from existing players might you expect?
2. What would you do to overcome these forces?
3. How might you remove the middleman to drive costs down?
4. How might you cut costs with a warehouse concept?

5. How might you improve turnover to allow less margin?
6. How might you combine discounting with choice to create a powerful double force?
7. How can you combine discounting with convenience?
8. What can you do to charge less for your goods and services?
9. How might you proactively exploit the discounting imperative?

Discounting is a fundamental force that will confront your business throughout the nineties. It can revolutionize an industry virtually overnight. Those who are complacent, who act as if they have a natural right to be in a particular business, usually do not react swiftly enough when the discounting onslaught strikes.

We have mentioned in this chapter and elsewhere that companies must add value to avoid becoming vulnerable on price. The specifics of the value-added equation are the subject of the next chapter.

VALUE-ADDING

Creating Alternatives to Price Competition

> *If you are totally customer-focused and you deliver the services your customers want, everything else will follow.*
>
> —ROGER A. ENRICO
> President, PepsiCo

VALUE IS SUCH an overused phrase that it's hard to be taken seriously when proposing it as a key to the nineties. But when managing the future, this otherwise trite word takes on important new meaning.

To manage the future, you must *add* value. In some cases, this means enhancing the products you sell. For instance, a computer store might integrate and install hardware and software from different sources. The new tested turnkey system has more value than the unassembled parts on their own.

But here's the key: You must *continually* search out ways to add value. Otherwise, value may provide a short-term benefit, but it cannot guarantee long-term survival. While you're patting yourself on the back, your competitors will imitate your innovation and come up with new ones of their own.

In this chapter, you'll learn how to turn value from a timeworn advertising phrase into a powerful, profit-boosting tool. We'll discuss the impetus behind this Driving Force and examine a half-dozen companies who have put it to work. We'll finish by looking at what you have to do to get this Driving Force on your side.

Why Value Is a Driving Force

Why is value so critical to success in the nineties? Because if a business chooses not to compete on price, then it inevitably competes on everything else. Continually adding value is the only surefire way to sustain competitive advantage other than offering the lowest possible price. Think of value-adding as the glue that keeps the customer coming back. It is the epoxy of customer loyalty in an era when customers are prone to wander off and not come back.

Sometimes service is part of adding value. But service is more than just friendly smiling faces at the front counter. It's both tangibles and intangibles, which form two aspects of the customer's overall satisfaction:

a) *Customer service.* Your people skills. The quality of the relations between you and your customers. Customer service is the subject of the next chapter.

b) *Value-added service.* The extras you provide. The additional services that distinguish you from the competition. Value-added service is one of the things we'll cover in this chapter.

While the two types of service are almost always mentioned in the same breath, they actually represent two different Driving Forces. Because they are often misunderstood, many businesses fail to capitalize on them. Indeed, some companies are aggressive at one, yet lax at the other. And some companies emphasize one type of service when they would be better off emphasizing the other. When only one is executed well and the other is neglected, the result is dissatisfied customers and a point of entry for an attacker. When both are well executed, the effect is unbeatable.

To understand the distinction between *customer* service and *value-added* services, consider the banking industry.

The courtesy and personal attention you receive from the clerks fall under the label of customer service. The new twenty-four-hour automated teller installed for your convenience is a value-added service.

With those definitions out of the way, let's explore how value motivates customers. When businesses do not compete strictly on price, the customer's attitude is always, "What have you done for me lately?"

"The consumer of the nineties will be the smartest consumer we have ever dealt with," observes futurist Laurel Cutler. "Despite the complaints about our educational system, we are training people to be very smart consumers."

Cutler is right. In the coming years, competitive advantage will come from delivering superior customer satisfaction by adding value. But rather than talk theory, let me give you some examples of what I mean. Let's consider a manufacturer, a retailer and a service business and look at a few of the ways they might add value. I think you'll quickly come to understand what I'm talking about.

For instance, a manufacturer could sell the exact same product as another but add value by offering:

- enhancements
- faster turnaround
- electronic ordering (so customer gets immediate confirmation, shipping date and inventory information)
- financing alternatives
- warehousing service (manufacturer stores and ships customer orders as needed)
- shipping options (express service when needed)
- point-of-purchase display materials

Likewise, a retailer—let's say a home center—could add value by providing:

- an information desk
- an answer desk for home projects
- in-store classes or seminars for customers
- manufacturer demos for interesting new products
- better signs so customers can find what they want
- computerized kitchen and remodeling planning
- free samples
- a greeter at the door to direct people to the right department

Or a service business—let's say a consulting firm— could add value by providing:

- a toll-free number
- a computer bulletin board customers can use to access rapidly changing data or instructions
- twenty-four-hour message and/or paging service
- desktop-published reports with graphics and charts for easier reading and understanding
- a free follow-up visit
- free phone consultation
- discounts on future services
- products for one-stop convenience
- laptop computers for instant, on-site analysis
- training classes, tapes, books, etc., to reinforce concepts

HOW COMPANIES PROFIT BY ADDING VALUE

Future-managing companies make it a point to know and cater to their customers' changing tastes. And they make it their task to constantly and continuously look for ways to add value to every stage of the purchasing cycle. Let's look at how standouts are cashing in.

AMERICAN EXPRESS. American Express's credit card division has adroitly managed the future because it understands what its customers value most: *snob appeal.* After all, Visa and MasterCard are accepted at more locations and provide the convenience of not requiring you to pay off the balance each month. The Discover Card actually pays you a small dividend every time you use it. So why does American Express keep gaining market share? Because American Express understands people's desire to feel special, unique, even elite. Which is why American Express continues to introduce a steady stream of new value-added services. Platinum cardholders, the elite of the elite, pay $300 a year for a bundle of high-end services. They can rub elbows with the rich and famous at the Centurion Clubs, a network of twenty-nine establishments in American, European and Asian business districts. They can call on the assistance of the Consul Clubs, which provide key business services such as language interpreters and fax machines to the traveling executive. They can tap a worldwide personal assistance network to locate hard-to-find items or even to take care of shopping needs. Among the Platinum card's newer offerings is a fine dining program that enables cardholders to obtain last-minute reservations at some of the nation's finest restaurants.

How does it know what new services to offer? American Express constantly surveys its members and conducts focus groups to avoid guessing.

FOUR SEASONS HOTELS. Four Seasons Hotels has been the innovator in introducing value-added amenities for its guests. It introduced the concierge service (now standard in most top-end facilities), twice-daily maid service, full secretarial and translation services, fitness centers and alternative cuisine lower in calories, cholesterol and sodium. Furthermore, Four Seasons was among the first to install a computer bank that stores information about each guest's personal preferences. Does customer Smith require a nonallergenic pillow? Does customer Jones prefer a rare kind of tea?

In targeting "sophisticated people who will pay more if they believe they're getting more value," Four Seasons wrestles constantly with the question of what its customers believe is value. "What do they want or need, or haven't yet realized they want or need?" asks John Sharpe, executive vice president. "What is it precisely that we're selling?"

In researching their market segment, Four Seasons put itself in its customers' shoes. "They are often under pressure while fighting jet lag, stress and the clock," says Sharpe. "They needed service that would eliminate hassles, help relieve fatigue, ease stress, save time—the luxury they were used to. But more important than that is a support system to replace the one they had left behind at the office."

With such attention to customers, it's no wonder that in a recent year, when the American Automobile Association presented its prestigious Five Diamond awards for excellence, Four Seasons, with ten awards, had more than twice as many as any other hotel group. Since going public in 1985, Four Seasons' net earnings and earnings per share have increased every year, as have revenues.

UNOCAL. In an effort to distinguish itself in the service-denuded gasoline market, Union Oil Company is positioning itself as a *service* station rather than a gas station. By emphasizing such value-added services as clean rest rooms, windshield cleaning and a check under the hood, Unocal is targeting customers "for whom their car is important and who are looking for more than gasoline," says a company spokesman. A print advertising campaign underlined the company's commitment by boldly picturing a squeegee, a dipstick, a rest room key and a tire valve—the traditional symbols of service. For those who want to pump their own, the company offers self-service as well and is installing user-friendly pumps and hoses. Unocal's philosophy is simple: "If customers believe they are really going to get better service, they'll pay more for it."

CIRCUIT CITY. Richmond, Virginia–based Circuit City has become the nation's largest and most profitable specialty retailer of consumer electronics and major appliances. The company accomplished this remarkable growth and profitability by defying conventional wisdom. It is a value-adding discounter. A contradiction in terms? How can the company provide both?

"What allows us to be both a discounter and a full-service retailer is our market share," says Richard Sharp, Circuit City's CEO. "Our share on the home electronics side is typically three to four times our nearest competitor's, generally in the twenty-five-percent range or higher. The combination of large market share, efficient operation and increasing buying clout has allowed us to become the low-cost, full-service producer." What allowed Circuit City to emerge as the low-price leader, Sharp explains, was the fact that when the chain was just starting, most of its competition was from department stores and mom-and-pop retailers. "They all had substantially higher cost structures than we did because they were full-service retailers. That gave us an initial foothold. You have to remember that pricing is always relative to the predominant competition."

If the predominant competition used to be department stores, isn't Circuit City vulnerable to the warehouse club discounters? "To a certain extent, maybe," Sharp concedes, "since they have a cost structure that is substantially lower than ours, or any other full- or moderate-service retailer." But Sharp is convinced that most consumers won't seek to buy stereos and televisions and VCRs in what he calls a "zero frills environment," since "buying electronics is a fairly high-anxiety purchase. It's big ticket, high technology and consumers don't want to make a mistake. They want a broad selection, which the warehouse clubs don't provide. And they want knowledgeable sales counselors, which the clubs don't have. And just as important, they want to know that if they have a problem afterwards, that somebody is there to fix it if it breaks."

In its early days, Circuit City competed almost exclusively on price. Its new slogan is "Circuit City—Where Service is State of the Art." As Sharp explains, "In the earlier days our focus tended to be more on price. The prevailing attitude was that since we offered low prices the customer would be willing to tolerate a bit more inconvenience. But as I looked at where the business was going, I felt that with the two-wage-earner families and with the increasing affluence, that people would be less willing to be inconvenienced and would demand higher service levels."

The result was a rethinking of every aspect of the customer's purchasing cycle for ways to improve customer satisfaction. Out of this process came a more upscale store design as well as an increased focus on the entire customer experience. A typical Circuit City electronics superstore features more than 14,000 square feet of selling space and 2,800 brand-name items. Also contained within each superstore is a credit office, a warehouse, a car stereo installation facility (many discounters don't install), a sales training room and a service department.

In rethinking its business from the standpoint of its

customers, Circuit City came up with value-adding innovations at every turn. Typical example: product categories are arranged around a central "racetrack," a walkway that guides the customer through the store to individual selling boutiques. Bold, clear signs help customers find their way around. Each boutique displays products by price and features, simplifying the purchase decision while providing the breadth of selection consumers demand.

At least part of Circuit City's brainstorms came from studying the competition. "We had studied the catalog retailers like Best Products because they were some of the first discount retailers," says Sharp. "They were slow as molasses. You walked in and filled out this paperwork, you stood around for a while, then they called you to the counter and you paid and then they finally called you to the pickup area and you picked it up and they sometimes called you to the counter and told you, 'Sorry, we don't have this item in stock.' It was a frustrating experience. We looked at how much hassle the customer had to put up with and turned our minds inside out looking for better ways of speeding the customer through the purchasing cycle.

"I made the decision that we needed to commit the extra dollars necessary to have enough sales counselors on the floor and in the warehouse so the customer didn't have to wait," says Sharp. Features the customer doesn't see also add value to the purchasing experience. But even the best customer service in the world is disappointing if the customer can't find what he wants—or has to wait while the product is special ordered. Breakthrough solution: Half of each Circuit City store is devoted to warehousing the many product models it displays in its showroom. Result: The customer often gets *instant* delivery—whether it's a Walkman or a washing machine—even during peak selling seasons.

Finally, Circuit City looked for ways to add value in another arena of constant frustration for customers—in the after-sale servicing of products that don't work.

"We spent a good bit of time analyzing the best way to provide [after-sale] service," says Sharp. "The complexity of the product today, the cost of the parts inventory, the availability of technicians and the need for adequate supervision make it virtually impossible to have service departments at each store site. Our solution was to set up regional service departments. We have special vans with carpeted shelves that are used for nothing but transporting the merchandise back and forth."

While still offering customers a low-price guarantee, Circuit City has added value to every aspect of the purchasing cycle. The combination has proved to be a killer for competitors, and not just the small stores. Pacific Stereo, once a dominant player in the West Coast consumer electronics market, was run into the ground in the mid-1980s by Circuit City's juggernaut. The firm's ability to exploit not only the discounting, but indeed *all ten* of the Driving Forces of change, make it a formidable competitor in the coming years.

Independent Operators

From the foregoing examples, it might appear that adding value works only for large companies. Not so. Small companies have many advantages in their closeness to their customers and in their ability to respond quickly. Let's close this section, therefore, with some real-life value-adding experiences from the world of small business.

And just how does a small business defend itself from the big companies with their deep pockets? By outthinking them in the change department, that's how. By creatively adding value to strengthen customer loyalty. By offering personalized services and extras that the biggies can't.

Huntington Market, in affluent San Marino, California, is one of a small number of independent grocers who have not only survived, but thrived in a region of intense price competition and aggressive supermarket chains. With a single phone call, Huntington Market customers can order a roast for dinner, slow-baked by the market's chefs. With a minimum purchase of other groceries, Huntington Market will even deliver at no extra charge. Observes Bruce Hotra, co-owner of Huntington Market, "There are things you can do, services you can offer in a market our size that you can't do in a large supermarket."

Smaller companies can thrive by being more nimble. Take independent bookstores. In the late 1970s, they seemed to be going the way of independent hardware stores and independent drugstores—into the dustbin of retailing history. Even department stores stopped carrying books, unable to compete with the more efficient chains. With nearly 7,000 outlets, the bookstore chains grew to account for half of all books sold in the United States.

In the face of new and flashier chain outlets from Waldenbooks, B. Dalton's and Crown, independents were boarded up by the dozen. But then some of them got busy managing their futures. They asked, "What can we offer customers that the chains don't or can't?" The chains could rightfully take credit for expanding the overall market by attracting customers in shopping malls who might never have sought out an independent bookstore. On the other hand, the independents began to realize they had values that the chains didn't. Many customers weren't wild about the impersonal self-service, limited selection, rapid turnover, bestseller-driven environment of the chain stores.

By acting to preserve their unique values and by adding new ones, prescient booksellers not only survived but flourished. Their customers prefer browsing in a homey, warm environment, so they have consciously enhanced that environment. Some have even added comfortable chairs and fireplaces. Here are a few of the ways independent bookstores are succeeding by adding value.

- *By providing a greater selection.* The typical chain bookstore carries 15,000 titles. Atlanta's Oxford Books has a selection of 125,000 titles. To give the customer more time to browse such a selection, Oxford stays open until midnight and until two A.M. on weekends and has a gourmet coffee shop that serves sandwiches and bagels as well as coffee and tea.
- *By searching for difficult-to-find titles.* At Tattered Cover, a Denver bookstore with 120,000 titles on the shelves, if you can't find what you're looking for, they'll find it for you, a value-adding service which 2,000 customers request each week.
- *By offering customer-coddling services,* including free gift wrapping (Odegard Books, Minneapolis), a quarterly newsletter for customers with listings of new titles and announcements of author signings (Tattered Cover) and charge accounts (John Cole's Book Shop, La Jolla, California). All add value in their customers' eyes.
- *By specializing.* Cody's Books caters to its high-tech Silicon Valley customers with a broad selection of esoteric technical tomes and with knowledgeable salesclerks who are computer whizzes themselves. And Pasadena's Scene of the Crime offers not only a superb selection of mysteries and thrillers, but also special events and mystery tours.

While some independents have rebounded, taking their eyes off changing customer tastes could quickly prove disastrous. One reason is that the chains, faced with the slower growth of shopping malls, are turning up the heat. Crown, the discount chain, is continuing its nationwide expansion. The two largest chains have published mail-order catalogs and promise speedy home delivery. Responding to the Choice Imperative, they've introduced frequent-buyer programs that offer member discounts, newsletters and new title updates customized to a customer's particular interests. For example, a frequent buyer of romance books might receive a newsletter and coupons for romance novels. "This is designed to generate customer loyalty," noted Waldenbooks' Ron Jaffe, senior marketing director, in announcing the program. The moral: Independents, like everyone else, cannot stop searching for ways to stay ahead by adding value.

PRINCIPLES FOR EXPLOITING THE VALUE IMPERATIVE

No matter what business you're in, managing the future means improving your business. Here are four principles you can apply as you seek new ways to add value.

1. Determine How Your Customers Experience Value

Companies that guess at what the customer values often miss. Singer, to cite one example, did not know its customers valued a simple sewing machine. So its engineers kept adding more complex features. Singer's sales organization wanted these features because they thought they would add value for the home sewer. But the sales force wasn't really in touch with the real customer. They were listening to selected resellers. By adding bells and whistles Singer was innovating for the wrong people.

Inventory how your customer realizes value from your products or services and from your business as a whole. Make a list of all the services you now provide that the customer values: your hassle-free-return policy, convenient hours, your wide selection of styles and colors, your willingness to customize solutions. What do customers like the most about you that sets you apart? What do your customers see as your unique strengths?

And now: What new enhancements would they appreciate that no one has offered yet?

2. Survey Customers Frequently

Formulate a list of key questions to pose to your customers. Make time in your schedule to ask at least ten customers the same questions.

Adding value isn't something a business does once or twice a year, and lets it go at that. It's an ongoing process.

Add the right things and you build customer loyalty. Add the wrong things and you may end up merely increasing your overhead or even alienating the customer.

American Express's ability to know which value-added services please its customers doesn't happen by magic. The company's extraordinary record comes from surveying customers frequently and then extensively testing and refining new ideas. American Express promptly drops ideas that don't add value in the customer's eye and constantly searches for new ideas. How about automatic car rental insurance? Or twenty-four-hour customer service lines? Amexco segments its customers based on lifestyle, demographics and income brackets. It adds value via services that appeal to each group: extra travel insurance for security-conscious seniors, a special magazine for students and so forth.

Even if you can't afford the expensive surveying system used by American Express, you can still create and administer simpler surveys that will help you keep a finger on your customer's pulse. For example, as a professional speaker, I am constantly surveying my audience. My customers are out there in front of me and I am receiving signals from them that I intuitively interpret as I deliver my service. And I long ago came to rely upon a more accurate way of determining customer satisfaction. Whenever appropriate I include with my handout material a simple survey asking the following questions: What was the most valuable part of the program for you? What should I, as your speaker, change/improve/add? and third, Please write a brief summary of the program's value to you. Then I ask each customer for a numerical rating on a scale of one to ten:

10 = Very worthwhile, I'm really glad I attended.
5 = Picked up a few ideas, but feel just so-so.
1 = Wish I hadn't come. Wasted my time.

This simple survey revolutionized my customer satisfaction levels. It taught me that a speaker cannot accurately gauge the customer's satisfaction level by how demonstrative or warm the audience is. Some audiences sit poker-faced throughout, yet give me the highest ratings and rave about the program on the feedback sheet.

Consciously seeking feedback can help you discover what customers really value. The two most important questions are 1) What are customers willing to pay more for? 2) How can I increase value while keeping the same price?

3. Listen to Your Competitors' Customers as Well as Your Own

Norman Brinker, chairman of Chili's Inc., is one of the country's most respected restaurant gurus. In a six-year period he expanded Chili's from twenty outlets to 194, generating $220 million in sales in 1988. His disciples have gone on to turn around such successful chains as Chi-Chi's and TGI Fridays. Shortly after purchasing Chili's in 1983, then a gourmet-hamburger chain, Brinker recognized that consumers were growing more health conscious. He quickly added salads, fajitas and grilled sandwiches to broaden his menu. More recently, he purchased Romano's Macaroni Grill, a San Antonio, Texas, restaurant, with the intention of expanding it. He had noticed that baby boomers had shifted away from cheaper fast food toward higher-quality restaurants with more atmosphere.

How does Brinker observe the changes in his customers' preferences? He likes to pose as a confused tourist outside his own restaurants. He asks departing patrons if they'd recommend it. He also visits competitors' restaurants, walking around like he's the manager, stopping at tables to inquire about the food and the service. "You have to listen to customers," he says.

4. Survey the Competition

Before Marriott launched its highly successful Courtyard chain, the company surveyed the competition. Much of its best information came from visits to nearly 400 hotels over six months. At each location, an "intelligence team" identified themselves as Marriott employees and asked managers about everything from employee morale to building design. Then Marriott took what it learned and invented a better mousetrap.

Sam Walton is America's greatest retailer. The first Wal-Mart opened in Rogers, Arkansas, in 1962. But not much happened until the company went public in 1970. Walton is known in the industry for his relentless analysis of competitors and for asking questions. He prowled New England, the cradle of off-pricing, and visited every discounter in the United States. He would introduce himself as "just an old country boy from Arkansas." The cornpone worked. One executive recalls bumping into Walton in one of the first K Marts to open in the Chicago area. "He was writing in a little notebook, and at one point he got down on his knees to look under the display cabinet. I said, 'Mr. Walton, what are you doing?' He said, 'Just part of the education process.' "

Adding value is essential for any company that doesn't compete on price. And, as we've seen from the example of Circuit City, it is increasingly important even to discounters. It can be doubly powerful when teamed up with customer service—a subject we'll explore next.

CUSTOMER SERVICE

*Building Competitive Advantage
through People*

YOU KNOW ABOUT customer service. You know what
it means. But you may not realize how powerful it can be.
Out of all the Driving Forces, only customer service can
single-handedly:

- overcome a competitor's price advantage
- let a small company take on a big one—and win
- build customer loyalty that lasts for years

Conventional wisdom says that customers make buying decisions based on logic and tangible factors: price,
features, options and so forth. But it doesn't always work
out that way anymore—as many businesses have found
out the hard way. In this chapter, you'll find out how to
put customer service on your side. I'll show you research
and real-life examples that back up my claims. And I'll
give you seven secrets that turn customer service from a
tired cliché into a powerful competitive edge.

CUSTOMER SERVICE AS A DRIVING FORCE

This book discusses the Driving Forces that are dramatically changing the American business landscape. But not
all of these forces are new. Some of them, customer
service in particular, represent fundamental values that

have re-emerged in importance. Here's why customer service has resurfaced, and why it will continue to shape consumer decisions:

1. *Today's harried lifestyles mean people value service more than ever.* People just don't have time for poor service anymore. Because today's consumers are more affluent and more time-strapped, they are also more willing to pay for service as a way to leverage their time. Households headed by thirty-five-to-fifty-year-olds will control 42 percent of household income by the year 2000. More than half of these households will have incomes of $35,000 and over (in 1985 dollars). "These people will demand service, and they will be able to pay for it," observes Cheryl Russell, editor of *American Demographics* magazine. "If they don't get it from your company, they'll get it from your competitor."

2. *Customer service is the surest way to differentiate a business in a look-alike landscape.* Competing department stores sell the same goods at the same locations. Competing airlines fly the same aircraft over the same routes while offering the same frequent-flier programs. Most banks offer nearly identical rates and services. How can you stand out if you live in one of these look-alike competitive landscapes? Answer: with the quality of the people who take care of customers.

3. *Customer service is the surest way to build and sustain competitive advantage.* The Forum is a Boston-based consulting firm that specializes in customer service. Its studies show that keeping a customer costs *one-fifth* as much as acquiring a new one. Other research shows that customers are *four times* more likely to quit buying from a company because of poor service than because they found a better or cheaper product elsewhere. The bottom line is this: Of all the Driving Forces, customer service is the surest way of building a lasting competitive advantage.

Unlike operational innovations, such as raising your Convenience Quotient or expanding your selection, quality service is much more difficult for a competitor to imitate. It is built over time by painstaking effort. Yet once you own the customer service niche in the minds of consumers, you have a powerful edge over competitors.

4. *Service is increasingly important, even for discounters.* As we've seen, price holds a strong allure for today's customers. But discounting alone may not be enough. Lower prices get taken for granted. Customers desert a discounter the minute someone offers a few more cents off. Since the inflationary 1970s, American businesses have been cutting customer-contact employees. For a while, American consumers went along pumping their own gas, fitting their own clothes and selecting their own products, from individual retirement accounts to stereos to computers. But even though we've gotten used to wandering on our own in stores devoid of clerks, we haven't learned to like it. Most of us never lost our preference for people. Result: Even successful 1980s discounters like Toys "Я" Us, Circuit City, and Wal-Mart have taken steps to bolster customer service for the 1990s.

Attackers vs. Defenders

Like all Driving Forces, customer service spotlights the difference between attackers and defenders. Attacking firms enter markets where existing players are complacent, where management has allowed itself to manage the past. They attack by distinguishing themselves so completely from the competition that their customer service becomes legend. The great irony is that *the power of customer service is lost on most businesses.*

Despite all the lip service, despite the constant boasts in mass-media advertising, most companies do not understand customer service. An example will illustrate my point.

A consultant recently told me that Las Vegas has become a battleground in the office products world. Within a few years a half dozen national superstores have opened there. With this kind of saturation, everyone is fighting just to stay alive. My friend recently visited several small Las Vegas dealers. At one store, the manager stood talking to him on the sales floor bemoaning the competitive situation and berating the local chamber of commerce for allowing the superstores to join. And, if you had asked this manager why someone should shop at his store rather than a superstore, he would have quickly answered, "Customer service."

But here's the irony. While the manager loudly aired his grievances for all to hear, *his customers were wandering around the sales floor completely ignored.*

So here's the lesson for the rest of us: Your customers must come first. Always. The way to win today's newfangled consumer is with old-fashioned service. To face the nineties and triumph, you must build loyalty—one customer at a time.

CUSTOMER SERVICE AS A REAL-WORLD STRATEGY

You know what I like the most about customer service as a battle plan for the nineties? *It works for any business, big or small.* Whatever their size, customer-service attackers have something in common. They understand the importance of putting the customer first and of truly living that philosophy on a day-to-day basis. Let's take a look at three of these attackers to see how they derive competitive advantage from customer service.

NORDSTROM. Most department stores don't hire salespeople, they hire cashiers. Thus, it's not surprising that
their attitude is, "If you want it, look for it, and if you
find something you like, I'll ring it up for you." But once
customers taste the Nordstrom difference, they are unwilling to make do with just a cashier. Nordstrom employees epitomize the expression "going the extra mile."
As the Seattle-based retailer expands into new areas, customers in those regions experience what we might call
the Nordstrom Effect. After this, other department stores
seem less impressive, more impersonal; their strategy
seems to be one of seeing how few salesclerks they can
make do with. Local men's and women's clothing stores,
unable or unwilling to tap the power of quality service,
find their customers deserting them.

In addition, Nordstrom combines superior customer
service with an unusual number of value-added services
free of charge: gift wrapping year-round; a no-questions-
asked return policy, which doesn't even require a receipt; one-salesperson shopping, wherein the same
Nordstrom employee can put together wardrobes with
pieces from different departments. Every Nordstrom
store has a fleet of "personal-touch representatives" who
shop on approval for persons unwilling or unable to
come into the stores. Since many people don't know what
to buy, the stores assign salespeople to help such customers find what they need.

In 1990, Nordstrom became the focus of several employee lawsuits and widely publicized charges by a Nordstrom union asserting that salespeople were required to
work off-the-clock writing thank-you notes and delivering purchases to customers. But then other Nordstrom
employees began petitioning to decertify the union as a
result of the controversy! Through it all, no one disputed
the fact that the chain's employees are the highest paid

in the industry and that the firm has grown at least 25 percent a year since 1984.

BUBBLING BATH SPA & TUB WORKS. Barry Fribush went into the spa business out of disgust, mostly. When his spa kept breaking, all he got were excuses from his dealer. It made him mad. "I figured I could do a better job selling and servicing them," he said. Along the way, he raised the standard for the entire industry. He did it by asking himself the question, "How can I make this experience better for the customer?"

The best spa is one that never breaks down and therefore requires no after-sale customer service. Having experienced firsthand the problems with cheaply made spas, Fribush decided to sell only those with a proven track record for reliability. To make sure the customer doesn't get a lemon, he tests every spa before a customer ever jumps in. A former road manager for several well-known Motown musical groups, Fribush used his working knowledge of electronics to create a sturdier installation kit than was available.

But no product is perfect and eventually even Bubbling Bath spas needed servicing. So Fribush looked at ways to improve customer service. As an owner, he'd had his fill of poorly trained, unprofessional technicians who kept coming back because they didn't fix it right the first time. He also noticed that arranging house calls was inconvenient. Most spa repair people worked nine to five. They went home with the rest of the workaday world.

That didn't make sense from the customer's perspective, since the vast majority of service requests come between four and seven P.M. That's when people come home from work, flip on the spa and find it isn't working. It stood to reason that this was when you needed to have service people ready to respond—so Fribush made it so.

He further strengthened his competitive advantage by guaranteeing to respond to all service requests in four hours or less. And before those service people rolled out, Fribush made sure they knew what they were doing. Rule one: All service people must own a spa, which Fribush sells to them at cost. That way they know the product from the user's standpoint. But Fribush still had problems, especially finding good service people. His innovative solution: Since he was hiring them for evenings on a part-time basis, Fribush recruited repairmen who worked during the day fixing copiers and computers for companies like IBM, Xerox and Honeywell.

"Since most spas today are computerized," explains Fribush, "there's not a lot of difference between fixing the control panel for a copier and one for a spa. By hiring these people I not only get people with excellent mechanical skills—they wouldn't be working for Xerox unless they were good—*but they also have been trained in how to deal with the public.* What I look for in everybody I hire is whether they are good communicators. They may be the best technician in the world, but if they don't have good communication skills, they can't work here." Then, because they were only working part-time, he could pay them more, up to three times what his competitors pay service people.

Bubbling Bath's approach to selling on service doesn't cost, it pays. Fribush estimates that 65 percent of his sales are spurred by his reputation for excellent service. He has a dozen competitors within a five-mile radius, but Fribush's company services everything sold by his competitors, only two of which have service departments.

Because Barry Fribush had the vision to manage the future, he raised the standard for an entire industry. Perhaps because he was an industry outsider when he founded Bubbling Bath, he did not accept the way things were. Sometimes the essence of customer service is figuring out how to minimize the need for follow-up service. And then, when it is necessary, making the experience so impressive that your customers become your unpaid sales force.

BRITISH AIRWAYS. In the 1990s, British Airways employees made being aloof, cold and uncaring a new art form. The entire organization was a bureaucratic swamp. Employees were unmotivated and customers were angry. By 1983, things had reached such a low point that employees were embarrassed to say they worked at British Air. Then, as a result of a dramatic management shake-up, British Airways asked customers for feedback. New CEO Colin Marshall took a novel approach. He asked customers what they wanted the airline to change. The surveys showed that, if the goal was building goodwill, a friendly staff was twice as important as operational factors such as food service, spiffy cabin interiors or speedy check-in. What mattered most to customers, after safety concerns, was how the employees responded to them as people.

So British Airways set about trying to convince its 35,000 employees that travelers should be treated as individuals, not cattle. They spent millions on training. And they pushed decision-making down to the local level to get lower-level employees involved in making improvements.

With customer service ingrained, the company next focused on value-added services, adding such niceties as wider seats, footrests and expanded menus and wine lists. The combination of customer service and value-added service has led to a doubling of revenues since 1987. British Airways is now ranked top in service in a poll by the International Foundation of Airline Passengers Associations.

HOW TO MAKE CUSTOMER SERVICE SERVE THE BOTTOM LINE

Nordstrom, Bubbling Bath Spa and British Airways might seem at first glance to have nothing in common. But looked at more closely, it's clear that all three have exploited customer service as their key source of competitive advantage.

Would you like to put customer service on your side? If so, follow the seven steps I've outlined below. They come from my research and interviews with executives who have made this Driving Force into a competition-crushing weapon.

1. Improve Service from the Top Down

Creating excellent customer service isn't something that can be achieved simply by sending the troops off to a smile-training seminar or two. It must be endemic to the entire organization, beginning at the top. If the leader puts the customer first, the company's service programs will have a much higher chance of success.

Too many executives believe they can manage and motivate employees as they did in the past. They are underpaying their people in a vain attempt to keep profits up, rather than looking at the true sources of profitability. They labor under the belief that they can still get away with providing the poor service customers tolerated in past years. Meanwhile, the world keeps changing. Their customers have more and more opportunities to bypass their products and services.

You can't blame poor service on the clerk who is desperately trying to figure out a complex electronic cash register while customers wait in line. The clerk obviously hasn't received the proper training. You can't blame poor service on the automobile salesperson who's been taught to hard-sell the innocent victim who happens to step into the dealer showroom; the problem is with management. You can't even blame the receptionist who answers the phone after the tenth ring and then puts the caller on hold while she leisurely pages the person called; the problem is with management.

Employees don't know the basics because management hasn't bothered to spell them out. Why? Often it's because *management itself doesn't know the basics.* The leaders haven't established standards for how the customer should be treated. All too often, employees don't receive a word about what is expected of them or how to make customers happy.

Ultimately, employees communicate to the customer how they feel about their jobs. If your people are happy, they'll make customers happy. (And if they're unhappy, they'll communicate that, too.) If your associates are not only happy but also receive periodic suggestions and training on customer relations, they'll make customers *very* happy. And all that has to start at the top. Or it won't work. Period.

2. Create Measurable Customer-Service Goals

For a strategy to work, it must have "buy-in" from the top team. If customer service is to be your competitive weapon, take your top people on a retreat and map out your service strategy.

A service strategy is a game plan in which you spell out the level of service you intend to provide. Most businesses never take the time to do this. To be effective, a service strategy must define specific expectations. How many rings before a phone must be answered? How many hours (or days) can pass before a customer query is answered? What do you say to the customer if the product fails? How much authority do you want to give your customer-contact associates? Have your team visualize key customer-contact positions from the standpoint of how those persons are to be taught what they need to know to carry out the strategy.

A successful service strategy must be simple, clear and to the point. The larger the organization, the simpler the strategy. At Wal-Mart, for example, employees are asked to take the Wal-Mart pledge: "I solemnly promise and declare that every customer that comes within ten feet of me, I will smile, look them in the eye and greet them, so help me Sam."

3. Recruit a Customer-Centered Team

With your strategy in place, you must find the right people to execute it. Trying to change a person's basic nature is close to impossible. People either like to deal with people or they don't. And while both introverts and extroverts can play useful roles, the trick is to hire people-lovers for customer-contact positions.

If you can attract and retain good people, you will excel at service. Check with previous employers for insights into applicants' people skills and their ability to resolve problems in a win-win fashion. Create a scenario with an imaginary rude customer, then ask, "What would you do in such a situation?" Do their answers jibe with your service strategy?

Those people who enjoy serving others form the real labor shortage of the nineties. Recruiting people who work well with customers, who understand what makes people tick and who can intuitively sense what will satisfy each individual customer's needs—that's the "rocket science" of many businesses.

4. Train Your Team in the Care and Feeding of the Customer

It's not enough to define your service strategy and recruit the right people. You have to dream up ways to keep the strategy alive in the minds of associates, so it influences their behavior every day. What's often needed are innovations in the way employees are trained.

When Toyota Motor Corporation introduced Lexus, management fretted that its $3 billion investment would stall in the hands of an ill-mannered sales force. What to do? How to make the buying process as refreshingly superior as the automobile itself? Toyota's solution was to make car buying an experience.

The company built its showrooms to exacting specifications. It was no less demanding when it came to the people it hired to sell Lexus cars. It picked from the cream of the crop, choosing mainly those with previous auto-sales experience. To reshape their thinking, Toyota came up with the idea of a Lexus boot camp. At the revivalistic two-day events, new salespeople were imbued with knowledge and enthusiasm through lectures, quizzes and role-playing.

As Lexus understands, interpersonal skills are not the only things customers value. Also important is at-the-fingertips product knowledge. The only thing better than friendly, courteous employees are friendly, courteous employees who *know their stuff.*

Home Depot, America's largest home-repair chain, discounts 30,000 items. But Home Depot's secret weapon is not low prices but its knowledgeable sales staff, known for giving good advice to novice do-it-yourselfers.

It's no accident that Home Depot's sales staff knows its stuff. Before Home Depot opens a new store, every new hire receives *four weeks* of training in customer service. Home Depot managers comb job applications to find workers with experience in the building trades and retirees with lifetime experience in home repair. Home Depot hires salespeople at well above minimum wage and beginning at the assistant-manager level, they are eligible for stock options.

Home Depot's training registers on the bottom line. Its 118 stores nailed down $2.8 billion in sales in 1989 and it expects to triple in size over the next four years.

5. Give Your Team Incentives to Provide Exceptional Service

So now you've recruited and trained a customer-focused team. The problem is, most employees get paid the same whether they treat the customer like a king or a jerk. They get paid the same whether the customer buys something or walks out. They get paid the same whether they fix the problem the first time or the third. But not at companies that are managing the future. The best way to ensure excellent customer service is to design your compensation structure so that everyone has a direct stake in the profitability of the firm.

Bubbling Bath Spa & Tub Works gives its service repair technicians incentives to do repairs right. As a condition of employment, all service technicians agree that if their repair work doesn't solve the problem, they'll go out a second time—but they won't get paid for the return trip. Before owner Barry Fribush instituted the policy, three out of every ten repairs had to be done again. Now the company gets only six callbacks a year!

This is an example of achieving results by rewarding the behavior you want. Future-focused leaders are creating all sorts of incentives. These include pay-for-performance plans, profit sharing and cash for good ideas. Of course, not all incentives are monetary. The most important incentive is recognition, as numerous studies have shown. Recognition is more of an attitude than an awards program. It is not something that happens only at the end of the year; it must happen all year long.

Conventional wisdom holds that commissioned salespeople create negative feelings by pressuring people into buying things they don't want. Yet Nordstrom's salespeople all work on commission. Until recently, most salesclerks did not. Seeing Nordstrom's super success, many have switched to commissions.

6. Empower Your Team to Solve Problems

Customers judge your company in two distinct ways: 1) how it does business under normal circumstances, and 2) how it responds when there's a problem.

Most organizations shackle employees with strict rules that don't give them the freedom to solve problems. To provide exceptional customer service, you must give your people the latitude to make decisions on the spot, even when the manager isn't around. It may cost you more in terms of mistakes and overly generous decisions, but you'll make up for it by strengthening customer loyalty. Observes SAS chairman Jan Carlzon, "To get new customers has a price, but to keep satisfied customers is almost without cost. On the other hand, it costs a small fortune to get dissatisfied customers back. So the danger is not that employees will give away too much. It's that they won't give away anything—because they're afraid to."

Some examples: Sewell Cadillac in Dallas allots service managers $50 per customer to make things right for that customer. Nordstrom's return policy puts the locus of control almost totally in the hands of salespeople: "Use your best judgment," they are instructed. And on it goes.

It's a good idea to periodically review your return and warranty policies. A lot of policies and procedures are written for the sake of the organization and not the customer. The fewer rules that stand between the customer and your associates' ability to be flexible, the better.

7. Encourage and Reward Heroic Acts for the Customer

One of the best ways to keep your people living the service strategy is to reward them when they go beyond the call of duty. Allow me to share my favorite hero story.

Not long ago I was invited to keynote the Association of Washington Cities' annual convention in Spokane, Washington. I did something that every frequent flier knows better than to do—I checked a bag. I got to Spokane, but my bag didn't. Since I'd arranged to arrive early, I wasn't too concerned at first.

By four o'clock the airline still couldn't confirm that my bag would arrive at all, much less when. So I grabbed a cab for Nordstrom. I'd phoned ahead to explain my predicament and to see if there was any possibility of having a suit altered on such short notice. Patti Riley not only helped me pick out a new outfit, but she surprised me with an example of service excellence that I shall not soon forget.

After making a mess of the men's department in helping me find just the right suit and accessories, Ms. Riley learned the alteration wouldn't be completed until nine that night. She was scheduled to go off duty at six. Realizing that I'd need the suit before the store opened in the morning, she volunteered to return to Nordstrom on her own time, pick up the suit and personally deliver it to my hotel.

That's what I mean by an heroic act. Question: When was the last time someone at your firm did something for the customer that was truly beyond the call of duty? How are you encouraging and rewarding this kind of behavior?

So there they are; I've just given you seven steps any company can take to breathe new life into its customer-service operation. But don't think I'm pretending that service excellence is easy. I have been able to boil it down to seven steps, but those steps are tough ones. They require dedication, commitment and patience. Customer service seems the simplest of all the Driving Forces. In reality, it is the hardest to harness.

You can look at this difficulty in two ways. You can choose to see the glass as half empty or half full. If you're a "half empty" pessimist, you'll complain about the time, trouble and money it costs to make customer service a reality. If you're a "half full" optimist, you'll realize the opportunity that lies in front of you. Your competitors face the same tough challenges. If you can succeed where they have failed, you'll have an advantage that's hard to overcome.

Looking for other competitive advantages in addition to customer service? During the past few decades, many companies have found them by applying new technologies. In the next chapter, we'll see the safe ways to profit from technology so the leading edge doesn't become the bleeding edge.

TECHNO-EDGE

Using Technology to Lead the Field

It's [hand-held computers] an absolutely critical strategic innovation.

—ROGER A. PODWOSKI
Vice President, Federal
Express Corp.

If you're a small business today and you don't have a fax, you're nothing.

—CASEY DWORKIN
General Manager,
Personal Technology
Research
Waltham, Massachusetts

This [inventory control] system is our greatest competitive advantage. We deal with toys but we do it with high technology.
—CHARLES P. LAZARUS
Chairman, Toys "Я" Us

THE YEAR WAS 1805. England lived in fear of an invasion by the Corsican upstart Napoleon Bonaparte. All that stood in Napoleon's path was a strip of water known as the English Channel. Then, at Trafalgar, in what became the decisive battle of this Napoleonic war, the British unveiled a secret weapon.

Up to that point, ship captains had to follow a rigid plan that they had agreed upon long before battle. If there was a need to change the plan in the middle of a battle, the captain was out of luck.

Then came Britain's techno-edge. They introduced signal flags so the battle commander could communicate swift changes in tactics. The flags enabled the British fleet to cover vast expanses of ocean, looking for the enemy, while remaining in close contact with the fleet commander.

Today, signal flags seem like an obvious advantage. Why didn't Napoleon have them? Perhaps because everybody on his team believed they already had the right stuff to whip the British: bigger vessels, bigger cannons, more ships, more men. Yet these advantages weren't enough. As a result of the signal flags techno-edge, the British achieved the undisputed rule of the seas.

This chapter is about how to beat the competition with the modern-day equivalent of the signal-flag advantage—with technology that lets you communicate quickly, respond rapidly and overcome the odds. And let's be clear on one thing: A techno-edge can come from any "tool." It doesn't have to be a computer. It could be a Polaroid camera, a fax machine or a color copier. It could be software you've developed or discovered, or it could be a gadget that's been around for years that you found a new use for.

A techno-edge can come from something as obvious as a cellular phone—but used in a less-than-obvious way. For example, most plumbers in Santa Barbara are sole proprietors. They have answering machines or answering services to take their calls when they are out. A customer whose kitchen is flooded by a broken water-filtration system is met with a recorded voice or an impersonal answering service.

Unless that flooded homeowner calls Bill Tharp of B-D Plumbing. Tharp carries a portable cellular phone, even when he's crawling around under houses. Tharp says that other plumbers now have cellular phones in their vehicles—but that's where they leave them! They use them to call their answering services. Those plumbers are not thinking from the customers' standpoint. Tharp realized that customers want to talk to a real live plumber who can tell them whether and when he can respond to their problem. So Tharp used technology to make it happen.

Bill Tharp's techno-edge is not the cellular phone. It's the way he *uses* it to add value. His competitors use their cellular phones to make their lives more convenient. Tharp uses the same technology to make life easier for the customers.

And that's the definition of the techno-edge. High tech or low, big business or small, it means using a tool to give customers more of what they want.

WHY TECHNOLOGY IS A DRIVING FORCE

One of the most significant changes of the past decade—and one that will relentlessly shape the 1990s—was the explosion of technological innovation. That explosion increased expectations. People expect computers to become faster, cheaper, more powerful. They expect television to improve in clarity, definition and sound. They expect software to become easier to use. And if company A can't deliver, they'll go to company B. If an American company can't deliver, they'll find a foreign one that can. To give the customer the same as you gave him yesterday is to give him less.

Technology drives change in other ways as well: It can change industries, alter long-standing relationships and create new forms of competition overnight. Take the newspaper industry, for example. Many newspapers have been in a severe slump in recent years due, in part, to advertisers bypassing them altogether. Instead, many advertisers are opting for other forms of media, such as direct mail, telephone marketing and catalogs, all of which tap sophisticated technology to precisely target today's fragmented populations.

Or consider the retailer–manufacturer relationship. Prior to the introduction of scanners (computer systems that record every purchase) in the past decade, retailers relied upon manufacturers to tell them how each product was performing. Now they can do this themselves. The balance of power has shifted. Many retailers now make manufacturers pay to keep new or underperforming products on shelves. Since they know exactly what's selling and what is not, retailers are quick to replace slow movers with competing brands. This shift occurred over five short years, changing decades-old traditions. Many manufacturers were caught off guard.

What happens when a company resists new technology? Just ask NCR, the cash register company. When electric registers first became a possibility in the early seventies, NCR decided to ignore them. Result: NCR watched as electromechanical cash registers went from 90 percent of the market in 1972 to 10 percent in 1976.

For NCR the wait-and-see approach proved nearly fatal. Twenty thousand workers at its obsolete electromechanical plants lost their jobs. The company was forced to write off $200 million in obsolete equipment. The chairman of the company was ousted by the board of directors. The new chairman put twenty-eight of thirty-five corporate officers permanently on consultant status.

In the 1990s, there will be other NCRs. The trick is not to be one of them.

To lead the field, you must continually use technology as a strategic weapon. In a moment, we'll take a look at ways you can make technology part of your battle plan.

But first, let's look at companies that have used technology to manage the future.

WINNERS ON THE TECHNO-EDGE BATTLEFRONT

Rarely is the demise of a business blamed directly on "failure to implement new technology." Instead, reports say the business filed for bankruptcy because it "did not control costs," or "overpriced its merchandise," or "took on too much debt." But often the insiders know that the business went under because the competition had a techno-edge that was as big an advantage as the signal flags at Trafalgar.

To lead the field, you must continually use technology as a strategic weapon. Attackers use technology to revolutionize how they serve customers, find new ones and lower costs. What follows are the stories of five companies that used a single technology—the computer—to develop a unique techno-edge.

AMERICAN AIRLINES. The original intent of American Airlines' Sabre computer reservations system was to make writing tickets faster and easier. But soon after American installed Sabre computer terminals on travel agents' desks around the country, it discovered that it had a potent weapon on its hands. American had designed Sabre so that its own flights came up first on the screen. Result: Travel agents, being human, tended to book the top-listed American flights for their clients. Sabre, combined with American's pioneering frequent-flier program, helped the company gain market share, from 12 percent in 1980 to 18 percent by 1990.

Even after the federal government required American

to rewrite its software to eliminate bias toward any particular airline, Sabre has remained a techno-edge. In 1985, the system contributed more to American's profits than did its regular airline business. In the final quarter of 1987, when the airline dipped slightly into the red, Sabre made so much money that American's chairman, Robert Crandall, quipped that, if forced to choose, he'd sell the airline and keep the computer system. Sabre's total value may now be as high as $1.7 billion, according to the company's estimates.

Sabre also enhances American's yield management, what the airline charges for each seat and under what restrictions. American's competitors watched aghast at the precise way American led People Express to an early grave in the mid-1980s with selective-fare wars. "If People had a three o'clock flight to somewhere," one competitor explained, "American would cut only its midafternoon fares to that same destination. If People was offering the fares on a limited number of seats, American would do the same."

Finally, Sabre is a tool that maximizes human effort. If the tray table on seat 2B doesn't work properly, the flight attendant can use the system to alert a repair crew to be ready with parts at the next landing. As one airline executive commented, "I don't think anybody perceived the crucial strength this system would bring to the party when American was building Sabre."

Maybe not, but that's often the way with a techno-edge innovation. Because American was willing to take a risk in its efforts to manage the future, it has climbed to the top of a highly competitive industry.

FRITO-LAY. A unit of PepsiCo, Frito-Lay first introduced its 10,000 delivery salespeople to hand-held computers in the late 1980s. Now they no longer spend hours filling out sales reports, orders and invoices. Instead they plug their computers into minicomputers at local sales offices or into modems in their homes. With the press of a few keys, their reports are transmitted to Frito-Lay headquarters in Dallas.

The company credits the $40 million system with saving $20 million a year through staff cuts, tighter inventory controls and a more efficient billing system. As with American's Sabre, unintended benefits accrued.

For instance, the hand-held computers help executives spot weak areas in their marketing. Before, if something went wrong in Atlanta, it often took headquarters four or five months to find out why. Now, management knows sales results twenty-four hours after the fact; they can see how many bags of Fritos, Doritos and other snacks are sold and to whom. The system allows managers to analyze how various brands are doing in every town and city. And it allows them to deal with problems through closely targeted promotions. As one Frito-Lay executive put it, "We have shifted our energies to solving problems instead of figuring out that we have problems."

WEYERHAEUSER. Tacoma, Washington–based Weyerhaeuser Company was an innovator in taking computer-aided design, or CAD for short, out of the engineering department and placing it in the hands of home remodelers. Weyerhaeuser's DesignCenter computer, operated with simple icons like those in Macintosh personal computers, allows customers to quickly produce custom-designed decks, wall-storage systems and outbuildings.

The DesignCenter sprang from an unlikely source. For more than a dozen years, Weyerhaeuser had used a computer simulation program to help its mill employees practice the best way to saw logs. Workers could cut up a three-dimensional computer-simulated log and the computer would repeat the process, showing the best way to do it. "We decided that since we had this technology, we should try to do something on the consumer level," says Bob Revell, project manager for DesignCenter.

The result was a system that includes a color monitor, custom computer, color printer and a tracking ball that allows customers to choose from icon menus. Customers first answer a question about their preferences: How high a deck do they want? How much of a load do they want it to bear? What kind of railing do they want? Within a few minutes, they can see a 3-D color image of the deck which can be rotated, analyzed and altered according to taste. The image even allows customers to "take a walk" around the simulated deck. The system provides a color printout of the deck along with construction diagrams and details. Another punch of a button and the system will print material cost information, including everything from the concrete for the footings to the lumber for the railing cap.

"The system is very simple," says Revell. "And the underlying time savings is the built-in engineering. It takes the parameters of the project and does all the work. When changes are made to the deck, the machine compensates instantaneously."

Besides speeding the time needed to design a deck and giving retailers a boost, the system corrected a recurring problem in customer–contractor relations. Through focus groups, Weyerhaeuser discovered that customers were often disappointed with their decks. "A customer would sketch out his plans, take them to a contractor and then, once the deck was built, would say, 'That's not what I wanted.' With DesignCenter those problems can be eliminated. Even building inspectors approve," according to Revell. "We designed our system to fit national building codes. But the ultimate official is the local building inspector. Never, to my knowledge, has a plan generated by our system been turned down on the basis of code. In fact, when people see the name Weyerhaeuser on plans, diagrams and lists, I think the plans have a very good chance of getting approved."

DesignCenter's mission is simple: It bolsters the demand for the raw materials Weyerhaeuser sells. But it's created a boon for retailers as well. "It's a sales tool that can be used to their [retailers'] advantage. Additional sales can be generated by a 'store module' that will call the deck designer's attention to related products such as paints and stains, barbecue grills and patio furniture. It helps make the store a one-stop shop for everything a person needs to build and outfit a deck," says Revell.

Weyerhaeuser also provides a four-hour training program for in-store specialists (called Champions) who are assigned to oversee the system. Retailers lease Weyerhaeuser's DesignCenter on an annual basis. Weyerhaeuser expects to expand DesignCenter nationally and into Canada by early 1991 and is exploring ways to enable customers to design additional home projects ranging from gazebos to room additions.

MRS. FIELDS COOKIES. There is more than cookies baking at Mrs. Fields Cookies. Since founding the company in 1977 and growing its sales to nearly $200 million, Debbi and Randy Fields have neatly divided their roles. Debbi's skills as an organizer and marketer keep the cookie company in the chips. Randy, a former IBM programmer, keeps the company in the know with computers and information systems.

Here's their techno-edge. They use Randy's technology to extend Debbi's skills and experience throughout the chain. The system is known as ROI—Retail Operations Intelligence. The name is somewhat misleading. It's more than just an information tool—it's an action tool for planning, scheduling, communicating and other business functions.

Each store, whether in Tokyo or Tallahassee, has a computer linked to headquarters in Park City, Utah. At the heart is an artificial intelligence expert system that allows Debbi Fields to project her baking and customer-relations ideas into every store in the chain. A Daily Production Planner, for example, taps historical data to project probable cookie demand every day, even down to the amount of dough that should be mixed in the Tallahassee store for a busy Memorial Day. Sales from all 650 stores stream into Park City every night. If there are problems, they are dealt with almost immediately.

Computer systems have helped Mrs. Fields keep its corporate staff lean and its organizational chart flat. All the operations of its 650 stores in six countries and its more than 8,000 employees are guided from headquarters where the corporation employs a staff of 115 workers in legal, financial, construction and other departments. There are no regional or district offices.

"The concept is a fundamental change in the way people do business," says Lavita Wai, Fields' director of product management. The deployment has been so successful that Randy is spinning off Fields Software Group, which will sell similar systems to other retail and service companies.

NOXELL CORPORATION. In 1986, Noxell Corporation, maker of Noxzema creams and Cover Girl makeup, introduced a new line of makeup designed to appeal to the growing legion of women over thirty. Then the company rolled out its techno-edge: a self-service computer customers can use to determine which shade of makeup best suits their skin.

The customer punches in the color of her eyes and hair and skin type. The computer then beams up the recommended shades of lipstick, eye shadow, blushers and base.

Noxell was not the first in the cosmetics industry to use computers. Other, more expensive makeup lines such as Coty and Charles of the Ritz pioneered their use in department stores. But Noxell was the first to take this techno-edge to the masses by putting its programmable units everywhere, including drugstores, discount stores and even supermarkets. The company more than quadrupled (to 30,000) the number of outlets where its makeup was sold. Noxell's breakthrough was not inventing the makeup computer. Rather, it was in making the computer self-service and placing it in stores where no salesperson was available. In one fell swoop, Noxell exploited four of the ten Driving Forces: convenience, discounting, age waves and techno-edge. No wonder the company's profits have been growing at an annual rate of 20 percent over the past decade and its market share in the mass market cosmetics business went from 15 percent in 1980 to 35 percent in 1990, the year it merged with Procter & Gamble.

SIX WAYS TO GAIN A TECHNO-EDGE

Conventional wisdom holds that technology-based advantages are difficult to maintain. Yet the companies we've just looked at demonstrate that the creative use of a technology (in each case, the computer) has provided and will continue to provide an advantage. Yet, despite all the hoopla over computers, most businesses are only now beginning to look beyond their simple uses—for "crunching" numbers and "processing" words. Only now have they begun to systematically look for creative applications.

Now that we've seen how a single technology spawns competitive advantages for companies as far afield as airlines and cookie shops, it's time to consider how you can develop your company's next techno-edge. So the critical question becomes: What's the next step in your evolution? How can you create competitive advantage from technology? Here are six strategies you can pursue.

1. Develop a Technology-Monitoring System

Don't leave technology to chance. Develop a systematic plan for finding and exploiting new developments. Whether you are division chief for a large manufacturer, president of a multibranch suburban bank or the owner of an asphalt paving concern, your industry has a techno-edge. Some company somewhere is state of the art. Businesses that discover and use new technologies before the rest of the pack are worth watching. They could provide a blueprint of your firm's future. Here are some tactics you can use to stay ahead of the pack:

- Start a new-technology file. Ask colleagues to contribute interesting articles, ideas and suggestions that might apply to your business.
- Attend at least two trade shows a year and pay particular attention to new technology. Or: Assign at least one person as your "technology scout," with the responsibility of reporting back to the rest of the team.
- Subscribe to at least one industry newsletter. Call the editor at least once a year to ask about his or her favorite new ideas.
- Meet every six months with your top team for the

sole purpose of reviewing technological developments and plans.
* Brainstorm ways to adapt new ideas. Ask your-
selves, What is our techno-edge right now? What
do we want it to be in the future? List the technologies the competition uses. Are these ideas you can
adapt?

2. Research Yourself and Your Customers

One of the characteristics of innovative companies is
their early adoption of new technology. In 1975, Wal-
Mart installed computer terminals in every store. Today,
the company's state-of-the-art system does everything
from tracking inventory to assisting in the planning of
new stores. Wal-Mart also has a satellite-based private
network to link the stores more closely and allow video-
conferencing.

Jack Levin, professor of sociology at Northeastern
University, classifies consumers in two distinct groups
based on how quickly they latch on to new technology.
Early adopters, says Levin, are the technology lovers;
high tech is likely to be their avocation as well as their
vocation. At the other end of the spectrum are the reluc-
tant or late adopters. They are not technology-literate
either out of fear, disdain ("Who needs a PC? I've got
my yellow legal pads") or indifference. They're always
waiting for the price to come down, the applications to
be improved or the next generation to appear. With
certain exceptions, businesses show many of the same
patterns as Levin found in examining consumer behavior.

Nevertheless, it's dangerous to adopt technology until
you have made a clear, hard assessment of your company
and your customers. Take a look at your customer base.

Will they eagerly accept the new technology you are considering? Or must they be coaxed along? Your target market will determine just how you implement your techno-ideas.

With any new technology, the acid test is whether or not customers like it and feel comfortable with it.

A&P, Shop Rite and Publix all experimented with do-it-yourself automated grocery checkout. Kroger tested a system that let shoppers run their purchases through an electronic scanner and pay a computer with a special cash card. "The technology worked fine," explained a Kroger official. "But we found that people missed seeing a human face at the checkout counter."

When Citicorp introduced automatic teller machines in the late 1970s, the move was considered extremely risky. As competitors watched, Citicorp took the risk that consumers would adapt to the new way of banking once they were familiar with the benefits (instant cash twenty-four hours a day).

Result: In three years, Citicorp's ATM network helped the bank triple its market share. Today, Citibank boasts that 80 percent of depositors use ATMs and more than half of all customers say they no longer need to venture inside the bank.

In managing the future, it is sometimes necessary to sell the customer on new technology. If the benefits are there, customers can be won over by properly informing, educating and training them, adopting user-friendly features and marketing the benefits of the new technology.

3. Base Technology Decisions on Results

In other words, don't let yourself get so dazzled by technology that you ignore the bottom line.

Would Apple Computer have ever gotten off the

ground had it not been for the two Steves, Steve Wozniak and Steve Jobs? It seems doubtful. Each Steve was gifted in a different area.

Wozniak was a technical tinkerer. He could not have cared less about serving customers. Jobs, on the other hand, listened to what the market was saying. Then he went back to the computer geniuses and motivated them to exceed what they thought was possible. All with the customer in mind.

A company needs both Steves, but the Jobses need to be in the drivers' seats. The reason: They can resist technology for technology's sake. Business leaders must study the latest technological tools and associate with people who can keep up to date. If the techies take over, watch out that the company doesn't focus internally on its impressive capabilities, rather than on satisfying its customers.

The company that takes its eyes off the customer, even if distracted by a tool it considers a techno-edge, is managing the past rather than the future.

The tool itself is seldom the real source of advantage. To put it another way, it's not the technology, it's the way you use it. Take, for example, the increasingly ubiquitous fax machine. How are you currently using yours to better serve your customers? Here's how three businesses would answer that question:

- Auto Body Menders, Inc., in Cheverly, Maryland, observed that mistakes in the resupply of car parts were costly and time-consuming. To speed accurate deliveries, the company includes photographs of the parts with its orders and faxes them between parts departments, estimators and insurance companies.
- Copywriter Kari Auringer, of Auringer & Associ-

ates in Dallas, uses a car fax machine to send last-minute revisions to her office. Two of her clients selected her service, in part, because she offers the ability to make last-minute changes in their print advertisements.

- *Business Month* magazine uses the fax machine to differentiate itself as "the first magazine you can actually have a conversation with." Each month, *Business Month* publishes a FaxPoll, raising questions about important business issues. Readers—top managers of midsize and larger U.S. companies—fax back their opinions. Then the publication responds, not only with poll results, but with columns and major stories targeted to their customers' current concerns. Not only does *Business Month* receive thousands of responses each month, many are appended with further insights and comments.

A techno-edge isn't always to be found in investing in the latest, greatest gizmo on the market, but in making better use of the tools you already have. In some cases, techno-tools can have the opposite effect as intended. If your headquarters' staff uses voice-mail to insulate itself from the field, a techno-edge becomes a techno-wedge. Ask yourself regularly: Are we getting the results we intended with this investment? How can we make better use of what we already have?

4. Use Technology to Challenge the Status Quo

When everybody in an industry begins to use a new technology, the early adopters lose their advantage. Everyone is back on a level playing field. Then the industry waits for somebody to come along, spot a new tool and apply it in a new way. That somebody could just as well be you.

A few years ago, Houston architect Gary Whitney took a hard look at his industry and didn't like what he saw. Competition for design work was keen in overbuilt Houston. Margins were tight and getting tighter. Whitney believed the situation had grown so serious that it was just a matter of time before some of the weaker players got knocked out of the game entirely.

Whitney noticed how technology had changed the business. Design firms had all installed computers to automate some of the drudgery. At first, that had given Whitney's firm a competitive advantage since other firms in town were still doing everything by hand. Spec-writing software and word processors had cut down on the number of people required to do the labor-intensive documentation. Computer-aided design had reduced the number of draftsmen. But after a while all the other firms were doing the same. The cost-competitive relationship among firms had hardly changed.

The more he thought about it, the more Whitney realized that the next techno-edge had to come from looking at the *design process* in a different way. Once he formulated the problem this way, the solution became obvious: Given that each function was as efficient as possible, the place to find greater efficiencies was *between* functions, not just *within* them. Up to that point, each function was separate. First, the programmer found out what the client wanted and handed a report to the designer. The designer came up with a sketch and handed it to the drafting department. Starting from scratch, the draftsmen converted it to their CAD systems, then to the documentation department. The spec writers, starting again from scratch, drew up the contractor's specifications. Whitney's breakthrough idea: Use the computer to tie all these start-from-scratch functions into a fluid, completely automated process.

First Whitney did away with all drafting tables. His designers no longer doodle on sketch pads, but at CAD workstations. And since designers' rough ideas are already a good start on the finished drawing, draftsmen no longer start from scratch. When they need conventional shapes, for such things as standard windows or doors, they pull them from the computer's memory. This part of the documentation work is also stored in the computer, so the spec writer no longer starts from scratch either. Before, improving things in one department had no effect on the other departments. But now, that's all in the past. Whitney's new firm generates profit at twice the industry norm.

Why don't we see more breakthrough ideas? The problem is usually not technical. It's that we are locked into "that which is." We don't brainstorm long and hard enough about "that which could be." This is the role of the leader. Figure out what you want to do and find the technology to achieve it.

5. Use Technology to Gain Information Power

Part of the success of Mrs. Fields Cookies is due to the company's unique techno-edge, its ROI system. But the company's leap forward was not made possible by personal computers networked to the home office. It was the ability of the founders to see the power of information.

Information, captured, stored, sorted and conveniently retrievable via technology, provides a strategic edge in the marketing and management of Mrs. Fields Cookies. Yet the power of information is often not fully exploited.

For years, banks have had all kinds of valuable customer information gathered in their files, information from checking account applications, auto-loan applications, mortgage applications, etc. But what good is this information unless it's used?

Imagine a bank that knows how many children a mortgage holder has and how old they are. That bank knows precisely when to offer the customer a tuition loan, a loan for a second car or another credit card.

By tapping just this sort of information, First Chicago Bank targeted a direct mail campaign to existing customers. Before: 98,000 mailings led to 150 loans at a cost of $500 per loan. After: 2,275 mailings produced 250 loans at a cost of $36 per loan. That's using technology to gain information power!

In addition, information is a tool for empowering your employees and raising productivity. Consider making the firm's information available to employees on a real-time basis. Morale and commitment increase as employees understand the big picture. Problems start getting fixed by the people who first encounter them, without explicit instructions from management. As information is shared, hierarchical organization gives way to work teams and "ad hocacies."

This is perhaps the biggest change in management since management was first recognized as a discipline. And it's driven by technology.

Formerly, middle managers were required as informational processing agents. Not anymore. Companies that continue to resist this trend will continue to lose out to those that embrace the future by using the latest information technology to enable their people to better serve the customer.

Since information is power, how are you using the information you already have about your customers? What additional information might be valuable to begin tracking? And how can available technology and software help you make use of this information?

6. *Automate the Low End, Personalize the High End*

Fast-food restaurants are already turning to labor-saving technology to drive down labor costs and increase the productivity of scarce workers. But what they have done so far will seem rudimentary compared to what they and other labor-intensive businesses will introduce in the coming years.

Already, McDonald's has introduced a grill that cooks hamburgers on both sides simultaneously. Domino's Pizza was the first to introduce the automated pizzamaker that simply requires the attendant to put the raw pie in one side and pull it out the other. In the near future, machines will fry hamburgers, pour and serve beverages, fry chicken and deliver drive-in orders to cars in about half the time and at about half the cost that human workers require.

In the nineties, businesses that compete on price will be forced to find ways to drive down their labor costs through automation. Businesses that compete on value will add people—at least at critical points in the customer's purchasing cycle.

Personalizing the high end will mean different things to different businesses, but basically it means having enough well-trained associates to be available when the customer needs them.

According to Warren Blanding, publisher of the *Customer Service Newsletter* and originator of the term "automate the low end, personalize the high end," as many as 50 percent of all transactions can be handled by interactive systems in which the customer accesses the database directly. Easiest to automate: order entry, order status inquiries and other standard entries. (Example: What movies is a theater showing and at what times.)

Beyond this, observes Blanding, since good people are hard to find, you will make them happier if you apply their talents on the high end of the business, where there is no substitute for a talented human being.

I've spotlighted six ways to ensure that technology stays in the forefront of your thoughts. As you explore these avenues, keep this caution in mind: If you don't exploit technology, you can be sure that your competitors will. The techno-edge is more than a way to gain quick, short-term advantage. More and more, it is a matter of survival.

Many companies see technology as a way to improve quality. But technology is only one of the quality-boosting methods at your disposal, as we'll see in the next chapter, where we discuss quality as the final Driving Force in the nineties.

DRIVING FORCE 10

QUALITY

Cashing In on Customer Satisfaction

Quality is the only patent protection we've got.
—JAMES ROBINSON III
CEO, American Express
Corp.

We have seen what better-quality competition can do to you.
—ROBERT STEMPEL
Chairman, GM

Our customers are not there to field-test our products.
—STANLEY GAULT
Chairman, Rubbermaid

With a washing machine, you just buy it, use it, and that's it—no maintenance. That's the ideal, and that's the way we have to go.

—NOBUHIKO KAWAMOTO
Senior Managing Director,
Honda

OF ALL THE Driving Forces, quality, by far, has received the most attention in the past decade. Why make it the final Driving Force? Because, in a sense, all of the other Driving Forces are reflections of, or are part and parcel of, quality.

Just how important is quality? Not long ago, the Strategic Planning Institute of Cambridge, Massachusetts, set out to find the single greatest key to long-term profitability in business. Their finding: *quality as perceived through*

198

the eyes of the customer. Businesses having low perceived quality averaged a 1 percent return on sales and lost market share at the rate of 2 percent a year. Those having high perceived quality averaged a 12 percent return on sales, gained market share at 6 percent a year and charged significantly higher prices.

Quality is a Driving Force that applies equally to service businesses as it does to those in manufacturing. It applies to the overall experience a customer has with a company, rather than just how a particular product is made. Here are some popular definitions of quality:

- "Quality is customer satisfaction."
- "Quality is a belief about the degree of excellence of a product or service."
- "Quality is what the customer thinks it is."
- "Quality is conformance to a set of customer requirements, which, if followed, will result in a product that is fit for its intended use."

In this chapter, we'll look at quality from the perspective of how customers perceive it in your business, and how you can improve it for bottom-line effects.

Why Quality Is a Driving Force of Change

Quality, like most of the other Driving Forces of change, is not a new imperative. But it is one that has re-emerged in importance. This increasing desire for quality has been noted in various surveys. Perhaps the most telling was one conducted by General Systems, a consulting group. In 1978, roughly 30 percent of respondents surveyed said that quality was more important than price. By 1989, over 80 percent said that quality was more important than price.

In the 1950s and sixties, demand for U.S. consumer products grew rapidly. Japan and West Germany were rebuilding their war-torn economies. But American companies began to cut corners. American managers began to tolerate shoddy workmanship—the door handle that came off, the seam of the new blouse that came apart, the toy that worked until it was dropped the first time.

Not that consumers ever got used to poor quality. It's that they began to believe that this was the best industry could do. And then came the attackers, namely, the Japanese. They didn't have any such assumptions. And they flooded the market with consumer electronics, machine tools, automobiles and thousands of other products, often at lower prices. In doing so, they changed the consumer's perspective of what quality can be. Now, affluent consumers worldwide demand not only quality, but also technological innovation.

American companies are learning that if their products are second-rate, customers will quickly turn to those that are first-rate. In a global economy, brand loyalty doesn't have the same allure it once did.

Another reason quality has re-emerged as a Driving Force of change is its linkage with another Driving Force—lifestyle. Put simply, given the time constraints of today's two-earner families, nobody has time to hang around repair shops anymore. Nobody has time to take things back when they fall apart, even if they are still covered under warranty. Quality, with its assumption of durability, appeals to people more today than in previous years. With the environmental crisis, constantly throwing away products and replacing them with new ones just doesn't make much sense.

Well, enough about what quality is and why it's so critically important an arena in which to seize the advantage. Let's look now at some examples of companies that have made quality their competitive edge.

EXCELLENCE THEATRES. For years, going to the movies was an experience attractive to large numbers of people. But with the rapid advances in home entertainment technologies (CDs, VCRs, large-screen televisions, cable, etc.), the wow factor of the big screen became less exciting. Add to that a growing middle-aged population, and more people staying home to watch rented movies than ever before. As a result, movie theater owners faced bypass competition that threatened their future growth prospects. Indeed, movie attendance decreased since the advent of the VCR, dropping from a peak of 1.19 billion patrons in 1984 to 1.08 billion patrons in 1988, according to the National Association of Theatre Owners.

The VCR and the rented video were substituting for an experience many patrons felt had deteriorated in recent years: sticky floors, long lines, overpriced snacks, poor sound systems and small, claustrophobic viewing rooms instead of auditoriums. How to lure audiences from the comfort of their entertainment rooms?

Chicago-based Excellence Theatres' response was to upgrade the quality of the moviegoing experience—to make it again worth leaving home for. "Our philosophy is that moviegoing should be an event," observes CEO Alan Silverman.

This 370-screen chain rethought every aspect of the experience from the standpoint of customer satisfaction—from the design of the auditorium itself to the concession stand menu. In retrofitting its existing theaters, Excellence installed bigger screens and added cushioned seats with padded armrests and cup holders. All new theaters are designed to be as wide as they are deep, to provide optimum viewing to the greatest number of patrons. Excellence invested heavily to improve sound quality. For its multiple theaters together, extra insulation between auditoriums was installed to prevent sound intrusion. They improved safety features for entry and exits from darkened auditoriums. They installed marble floors in theater lobbies and easier-to-maintain tile floors in the auditoriums themselves.

To please the palates of an aging and more discerning audience, they added such items as cappuccino, bottled waters and frozen yogurts to their menus. Even popcorn—America's official movie snack—has been recast with the health-conscious consumer in mind. A new vegetable oil lower in saturated fat is being used as an alternative to coconut oil.

Equally important, Excellence Theatres operates from the vision that while amenities are important, what really makes the moviegoing experience an event are the employees: the cashiers, ushers and concession-stand workers. No matter that many of them are teenagers in their first jobs. They receive thorough training in the art and execution of customer service. And their uniform tuxedos are a reminder that they are part of a high-quality experience. "Our goal," says Silverman, "is to convince the patron that he or she was entertained, not just by the movie but by the overall experience."

H&R BLOCK. Perhaps the biggest irony about H&R Block is the fact that its founders, Henry and Richard Bloch, began offering tax service as a free value-added service to their regular business of bookkeeping. But seeing the tremendous demand for tax preparation service, they founded H&R Block in 1955. Two years later, Bloch opened two additional offices in Kansas City and seven offices in New York. In 1958, they began franchising, a system that allowed for rapid expansion. In 1962, the company went public. H&R Block sold 75,000 shares of stock at $4 per share; since that time the company's stock has split fifteen shares for each original share. In 1990, the company dominated this fragmented industry, preparing one in ten tax returns filed in the United States and two in every ten prepared by professionals, in addition to Canada and other countries.

"Quality is an accurate tax return, thorough, complete and with all legal deductions and credits," observes Thomas M. Bloch, the company's president of tax operations and son of cofounder Henry Bloch. "Unlike a lot of services and products, much of what we do is based on perceptions. Therefore there must be a perception by the client that he or she has received such a tax return."

How does an organization with 8,000 offices and 40,000 associates around the world maintain this unsurpassed quality? Through constantly adding to its existing methods of ensuring quality. Here is a look at that formula:

- *Through extensive training.* Training begins in September with a seventy-five-hour tax course that is open to the public. From these courses Block hires new preparers. Company headquarters supervises all written materials and increasingly relies upon video to communicate about nontax issues, including client service. Everyone is required to attend annual update seminars, although new hires receive the most in-depth treatment.
- *Through internal checks and balances.* Every tax return is checked by two people in each branch office, both for mathematical errors as well as tax theory.
- *Through written guarantees of quality.* H&R Block offers a written guarantee of quality and agrees to accompany the client in the event of an audit at no additional charge.
- *Through incentives that reduce turnover.* A big part of quality in the eyes of some customers is being able to deal with the same tax preparer year after year.

Approximately 75 percent of Block's seasonal preparers return year after year. One reason they do is that Block gives them incentives to return that include attractive options to buy stock at less than market value.

- *Through measurement.* The company annually sends out a report card asking for feedback from a randomly selected group of customers. By measuring the rate of repeat customers, the company then analyzes why it moves up and down. It averages about 75 percent, but fluctuates based on changes in the tax laws.
- *Through management fieldwork.* Almost all of the company's top management spend time working in various field offices during each tax season, answering calls, preparing returns, troubleshooting.
- *Through focus groups.* These groups help the company design specific new programs and were, for example, used extensively to make the design and marketing of Rapid Refund as user friendly as possible.

Others have tried to emulate Block's formula, but with little success. One major reason is the company's consistent level of quality.

EARTH'S BEST. Definitions of quality change over time and are subject to customer perceptions and influenced by such things as scientific research and congressional studies. One of these is the increased media attention to the harmful effects of pesticides, herbicides and food additives. A 1989 Food Marketing Institute annual survey found that pesticide residue in food is the number one concern of food shoppers, overshadowing cholesterol, salt and fat. Eighty-two percent of those polled said pesticides are a "serious hazard to health." And a 1990

Louis Harris poll found that, for two years in a row, 84 percent of Americans would prefer organically grown produce; 44 percent would pay more for it.

The founders of Earth's Best, a Middlebury, Vermont, maker of organically grown baby food, are cashing in on consumer concerns about chemicals in foods. Brothers Arnold and Ronald Koss founded the company in 1987 after noticing a gap in the quality guarantees of mainstream baby food producers Gerber, Beech-Nut and H.J. Heinz. The company has benefited from such incidents as the Chilean fruit-poisoning scare and the linking of Alar, a ripening agent, to cancer and its subsequent ban. In addition, an Office of Technology Assessment study notes that infants and the elderly face the highest risk of nervous-system disorders caused by pesticides, food additives and other pollutants.

Earth's Best's twenty-one-item line of foods not only gives parents a new choice, but a guaranteed level of quality. Available in natural-food stores and mainstream markets, Earth's Best uses only growers who are certified organic, which means that they are reviewed by private certifying organizations such as the Organic Crop Improvement Association, which sets tough standards for organic crop production. Produce cannot be grown in soil in which any herbicides, pesticides or chemical fertilizers have been applied in the previous three years. The only drawback is cost. Earth's Best costs about twice as much as competing Gerber and Beech-Nut brands. "As the American public increasingly understands the vital link between food quality and health," notes an Earth's Best spokesperson, "they will readily grasp the importance of spending more on organically grown food."

TECHSONIC INDUSTRIES INC. This is a company whose motto might be "When all else fails, let your customers help you design your products." Between 1977 and

1983, this Eufaula, Alabama, maker of Humminbird depth finders for fishermen came out with one new product a year, sometimes two. All of them failed.

This left the single product the company had been founded on, the Super 60, to take up the slack. As late as 1983, it accounted for 97 percent of the company's $11.5 million in annual sales. Investors were getting restless and talking of withdrawing their money. What to do? New president Jim Balkcom, who'd inherited the company from its founder who had since died, was desperate. When Techsonic's vice president of marketing hired an advertising firm, the ad man started asking questions about who the customers were and what they liked most about the company's product. It turned out that Techsonic's brass knew precious little about them. The ad man suggested they spend $20,000 to hire a marketing consultant to hold some focus groups with fishermen to find out. Balkcom was skeptical about what the marketing wizards would come up with, but, "We needed to do something different," he said, "and quickly."

Market researcher Sue Symons went to work. Traveling to Atlanta, Nashville and Dallas, she located people who owned boats and loved to fish. Then she performed what she called vision interviews. While they reclined in easy chairs, she interviewed fishermen one by one about their fishing experiences. What was the best thing that had ever happened while fishing? she asked. What was frustrating about the experience? Gradually, she steered the conversations toward depth finders. What they liked, didn't like, what they were really looking for in buying a new one. Then she transcribed the tapes and pored over them looking for common sentiments. From this she designed questions for a quantitative telephone survey. In all, 1,800 fishermen were asked to rank the problems they had with depth finders. It was the first time this fledgling industry had used such sophisticated marketing tools.

Fishermen's number one complaint turned out to be sunlight. They had trouble reading the gauges on their depth finders in bright sunlight. Complaint number two: depth finders were too complicated. "Our conventional wisdom," said Balkcom, "was that fishermen liked to press buttons. We were wrong."

What emerged from the intensive customer research was the Humminbird Liquid Crystal Recorder, a device which combined the most popular features of existing finders with a high-tech difference. The LCR gives a digital reading, charts a contour of whatever's below and gives off an audible signal that alerts the user to fish or underwater hazards. On July 26, 1984, at the American Fishing Tackle Manufacturers Association show in Atlanta, the LCR was unveiled to thunderous applause. Balkcom and his team had hoped to sell as many as 25,000 of the new devices. Instead, by the end of fiscal 1985, they'd sold 140,000 units. Sales hit $31 million, more than two and a half times 1984 sales.

HOW TO PROFIT FROM QUALITY

1. Assess Your Current Level of Quality

What is the most pressing area of your business where the customer perceives a lack of quality? Is it the overall appearance of your business? The type of products you sell? Your sales force's lack of training and product knowledge?

Start by assessing the overall, day-to-day level of quality your customer is met with. If you're unsure, start by asking your customers what they think of your quality.

2. Design with the User in Mind

Since quality is in the eyes of the beholder, design your products, services and methods of doing business with the customer in mind. The future belongs to companies that pay strict attention to defining the real needs of customers, as opposed to imagined or presumed needs.

International consultant Kenichi Ohmae, head of McKinsey's office in Tokyo, tells the story of a Japanese home appliance company's attempts to design a better coffee percolator. Should it be of the Mr. Coffee variety? the engineers asked. Should it be larger? Smaller? What would give the product a discernible competitive advantage?

Ohmae urged the designers to ask different questions: Why do people drink coffee? What are they looking for when they do? "If your objective is to serve the customer better," Ohmae asked, "then shouldn't you understand why that customer drinks coffee in the first place? Then you will know what kind of percolator to make."

It turned out that the coffee drinker was primarily interested in—you guessed it—good taste. So Ohmae then asked the engineers what influenced the taste of coffee. Nobody had a good answer, so the team went off looking for insights. Their research found that lots of things affect the taste of a cup of coffee: the quality and freshness of the bean, the way it is ground, the way the water is distributed over the coffee, the quality of the water itself. But water quality made the biggest difference, and thus the product was designed with a built-in dechlorinating function. Moreover, a built-in grinder was installed so that all the customer had to do was pour in water and beans and the machine went to work.

This is the way smart products and services are designed—by starting with the consumer. It is also the way to manage the future. "If your only concern is that General Electric has just brought out a percolator that brews coffee in ten minutes," says Ohmae, "you will get your engineers to design one that brews it in seven minutes. And if you stick with that logic, market research will tell you that instant coffee is the way to go.

"Conventional marketing approaches won't solve the problem. You can get any results you want from consumer averages. If you ask people whether they want their coffee in ten minutes or seven, they will say seven, of course. But it's the wrong question. And you end up back where you started, trying to beat the competition at its own game. *If your primary focus is on the competition, you will never step back and ask what the customers' inherent needs are or what the product really is about.*"

3. Independently Establish Your Quality

Companies have appealed to consumers about their quality for so long that such appeals long ago began to fall on deaf ears. The question is how to communicate to your customers the level of your quality. One answer: through independent assessments of your relative quality.

Earth's Best, the baby foods company, advertises the fact that it was rated highest by *East-West Journal* for its organically grown ingredients, its taste, color and texture—and the fact that it comes in glass jars, which the magazine felt "have stood the test of time." Major corporations now compete for the Deming Prize and the Baldrige Award. But even if you're not on the Fortune 500, there are ways to establish your quality in the eyes of customers.

What does *Consumer Reports* say about your product? For example, local newspapers often rate restaurants and other "best" businesses in town. Make it a point to compete for these honors, and use them in your advertising.

As various studies have shown, unless you communicate your quality, the customer may not see you as you are (or as you see yourself). In one study in which the quality of two products was increased (without any communication of that improvement), study participants exposed to the higher quality levels did not have higher purchase levels, more positive attitudes toward those brands or higher intentions to purchase those brands in the future, compared to other subjects. The article concluded: "In order to be perceived as such by consumers, quality increases may need to be introduced with a message identifying that change."

4. Monitor Changes in How Your Customers Assess Quality

As we saw in the example of Earth's Best baby foods, the big three, Beech-Nut, Gerber and Heinz, have been slow to embrace the growing desire for organically grown foods. A similar situation occurred when Detroit's big three resisted embracing the issue of automobile safety.

The change in consumer perceptions began with Ralph Nader's exposé of GM's Corvair in the mid-1960s, which sent that rear-engine model to an early grave. In the ensuing years, government tests and consumer group reports of results of crash tests made the issue of safety one of importance to growing numbers of people. Insurance companies began charging more to insure cars with poor safety records than those with good ones. But Detroit's big three failed to capitalize on safety, citing the added expense.

Meanwhile, Mercedes, Volvo and, to a lesser extent,

Saab, had achieved a competitive advantage from their customers' perception of safety. Volvo, in fact, had spent millions boasting about its safety features in graphic, decidedly unpretty advertising featuring its cars, full of dummies, slamming into walls at high rates of speed. The upshot of these forces coalesced to produce a perceptual change on the part of the car buyer that all companies, including the Japanese, had to respond to. And Detroit plunged headlong into selling safety.

While Mercedes-Benz of North America began putting air bags in its 1984 models and had them in all models sold in the United States in the 1986 model year, GM's Cadillac line began installing them on all models in 1989. Chairman Lee Iacocca, a longtime air bag opponent, decided to install them in all U.S.-built Chrysler cars in the 1990 model year. Ford Motor Company's 1990 cars feature air bags as standard equipment on eight models and optional equipment on two and expects to put 1 million new air bag–equipped autos on the road in 1990. By the mid-1990s, Ford expects air bags will be standard equipment in every Ford and Lincoln Mercury car sold in North America.

"We see more and more importance attached to safety all the time," says Joyce Stinson of Ford's technical–regulatory public affairs department. "When someone goes into a dealership now, they ask questions about safety rather than about acceleration." "We're trying to . . . respond to what our customers are telling us," says Helen O. Petrauskas, Ford's vice president for safety.

By the time Detroit responded in the late 1980s, safety was no longer a source of competitive advantage so much as a factor that could no longer be ignored. And as Detroit discovered, perceptions, once entrenched, are difficult to change. The moral: Keep an eye on lifestyle and demographic changes in your target population and pay special attention to changing perceptions of quality. Government reports, news media scares, accidents involving your products or those of your competitors can all have an effect on the customer's perception. Even when the course of events seems to be turning against you, realizing that reality first gives you the chance to respond creatively, rather than having to react in haste.

5. Look for Ways to Make Your Products User Friendly

Apple's Macintosh was light years ahead of the other personal computers in terms of its user friendliness, a feature that added the most important value of all—the value of being usable and therefore useful to the non-technically oriented person. Most telling was the way Apple understood the sources of its competitive advantage and exploited it fully.

In one television commercial, a huge thick pile of documents are dropped in front of the viewer as the voice-over intones, "You can read these manuals and learn to use a computer, or [and then a small, thin manual plunks to the ground] you could read our manual and get on with using the Apple Macintosh."

Of course, the Macintosh isn't quite *that* simple, at least not if the customer wants to use it for publishing, communications and a host of other uses, but compared to the competition, it was by far the most user friendly. Steve Jobs, the creative force behind the Mac, seemed intuitively to understand the old adage that what the customer wants when he goes into a hardware store is not a drill but a hole. Ditto with computers.

While Apple was cashing in on the value its user-friendly appliances provided customers, IBM was content with less user-friendly machines and an image of

"Big Blue." Focus groups convened by the company expressed feelings that the company was "inaccessible," "intimidating" and its sales force content to take orders and not often involved in their customers' businesses. But as competition has heated up, IBM has had to change its tune.

Often overlooked when companies attempt to add quality to their products and services is the area of accessibility or user friendliness. Just look at the way modern buildings are designed. University of Southern California's Dana Cuff was intrigued by a question few designers apparently consider: How do architects actually imagine the people who will work, live and play in their buildings?

The short answer is: They don't. Cuff found that most architects simply never bothered to ask themselves whom exactly they were designing for, beyond the immediate clients who paid their fees. Instead, Cuff discovered as she interviewed leading designers, they design to impress their peers, or they design for how they *wish* human beings would behave or they design for some idealized future, overlooking the way human beings actually use the spaces they shape. Says one, "I do my work for me—there are no other people. My work is not about convenience, it's about art."

The result of just this sort of attitude has been a rising choir of complaints about modern architecture, violent objections from the actual inhabitants and users of the finished design, and growing friction between professionals and the public. Laments Cuff, "I feel that architects should ask themselves how they might actually feel in the spaces they contrive."

The extent to which being sensitive to the end user can advance a company's prospects is clearly evident in designs ranging from San Diego's Horton Plaza shopping center to the Apple Macintosh to Japan's goof-proof cameras. Perhaps the best examples of all are the Disney theme parks. Visitors from all over the world can feel at home at Disney's parks in Europe, the United States and Japan because of their logical layouts and multilingual signs and staff.

The larger issue here is how much the inaccessibility of a business, its products and services may be turning customers away. Given today's ever-accelerating rate of change, it's necessary to constantly re-examine the customer's experience of your company from the standpoint of user friendliness. Never underestimate the range of intelligence and experience levels, cultural backgrounds and even attention spans of consumers.

As we saw in the previous chapter, New York–based Citicorp began investing in ATM technology a full decade before many of its competitors—and achieved a techno-edge as a result. But before it invested millions in the device, Citicorp thought deeply about how to ensure that mechanical banking transactions were as simple as they possibly could be. How high should an ATM's keyboard be for the average customer? What size type should be used in giving directions? By testing consumer reactions in advance, Citicorp came up with a superior design.

Most ATMs communicate brusquely with users, commanding them to "INSERT CARD NOW." But Citicorp researchers found that this type of message, while popular with designers, frightened away all but the most gadget-prone depositors. What customers warmed to, says Lawrence Weiss, chief of the consumer bank's development division, was a friendly teller.

Not satisfied with success, Citicorp recently began replacing its ten-year-old machines with newer models that are still just as easy to operate, but have greater capabilities. They look like the older machines but have larger, touch-sensitive screens that display images in full color and replace real buttons with pressure-sensitive ones. The new machines also display the image of an oversized typewriter keyboard on the screen, enabling a customer to write a complaint or enter an address change.

Are you exploiting this aspect of quality?

6. Be a Watchdog for Quality

Stan Gault, Rubbermaid's chairman, was walking on a New York sidewalk in 1986, when he heard a doorman muttering and swearing as he swept dirt into a Rubbermaid dustpan. Gault was right in the middle of a conversation, but he whirled around and started grilling the man about why he was unhappy. Gault learned that the lip on the dustpan was too thick, leaving a dirt line on the floor. When he returned to Wooster, he told engineers to redesign the product.

Like Stan Gault, you, the business leader, must be the ombudsman for quality in your organization. As you communicate to your associates, give them examples of what you mean by quality as perceived through the eyes of the user of your products and services. Talk about the failures of execution and the ideas you and others have come up with for improving those lapses.

7. Keep Your Associates Up to Speed on How the Product Is Used

3M Corporation sends hourly workers on morale-building field trips to see how customers use the company's goods. One such team visited a local television studio that uses 3M magnetic videotape.

8. Listen to Customers for Incremental Improvements; Listen to the Visionaries When Making Breakthroughs

Listening is finally starting to catch on with some major manufacturers. For example, Ford now shows mock-ups to customers at new-car clinics while its cars are still in the early design stages. The company used to sound out customers only after the car was in final production. But Ford has to be careful because, while listening to customers is vitally important, it won't point the way the future is headed. As Fritz Mayhew, stylist of the Ford Thunderbird, points out, "If you slavishly follow what the customer says, you will produce today's cars. People have to feel a little bit uncomfortable about a design."

Likewise, in computers, Steve Jobs was asked where truly great products come from. He responded that they come from "melding two points of view—the technology point of view and the customer point of view."

"You need both," he continued. "You can't just ask customers what they want and then try to give that to them. By the time you get it built, they'll want something new. . . . They won't ask for things that they think are impossible. But the technology may be ahead of them. It sounds logical to ask customers what they want and then give it to them. But they rarely wind up getting what they really want that way." On the other hand, going into the technology lab and coming up with a new product rarely produces something that meets the customer's needs. "You have to merge these two points of view, and you have to do it in an interactive way over a period of time—which doesn't mean a week. It takes a long time to pull out of customers what they really want, and it takes a long time to pull out of technology what it can really give."

216

A FINAL WORD

Having read this far, I know that you are a business leader who cares about creating a future-managing company.

And now, having read all about the Driving Forces and having jotted down your own ideas as to how you can create competitive advantages from these forces, you face a choice.

The choice is whether you will act on your ideas, or whether you'll let your good intentions lapse. The choice is what you will do with the ideas you've gained from investing your time in reading this book.

No business consciously sets out to manage the past. No leader sets out to let it happen. Instead, it happens gradually. The world continues to change. Customers' needs continue to change. But the business keeps on serving up yesterday's ideas . . . until it's too late.

On the other hand, if you do decide to act on your ideas, you'll be joining business leaders like Stan Gault of Rubbermaid and Fred Smith of Federal Express and Leslie Wexner of The Limited and dozens of others who actively and aggressively manage the future.

If the message of this book could be boiled down to a couple of simple statements, they might be:

- *Create ways to get even closer to your customers.* Shoulder-to-shoulder close. Eyeball-to-eyeball close. Take a tip from Debbi Fields, president of Mrs. Fields Cookies, who visits her stores and gives away free cookies to get direct customer feedback.

217

- *Become a trend-watcher.* Borrow a useful technique from Robert Hazard, CEO of Quality Inns International, and keep a little box on your desk labeled "Trends to watch."
- *Introduce improvements constantly.* They don't have to be big things. Maybe it's a new program that saves your customers time, like Red Lobster's "Call Ahead Seating." Maybe it'll be something as simple as redesigning your monthly statement to make it easier for your older customers to read.

Or possibly it'll be something more sweeping: like rethinking your business from how the customer accesses it, the way Circuit City did, and redesigning your systems accordingly.

Or maybe you'll create a new choice for your customers like The Packaging Store did. Or maybe you'll come up with a dozen new ideas that will add value to your customer's experience, the way Four Seasons Hotels and Excellence Theatres did.

Big or little doesn't matter. It's all part of managing the future. And it all adds up to a better, stronger, more profitable company in the long run.

There is an expression that says, "The best way to predict the future is to invent it." How true this will be in coming years. I hope that, as a result of reading this book, you now feel better prepared to take full advantage of the ten Driving Forces of change, and I wish you great success!

NOTES

Driving Force 1: Speed

28 Four out of ten Americans report pet peeve is waiting in line: "Sure Ways to Annoy Consumers," *The Wall Street Journal,* October 6, 1989.

28 In 1967, testimony before a Senate subcommittee: "How America Has Run Out of Time," *Time,* April 24, 1989.

28 The "Harried Household" study was produced by SRI International's Business Intelligence Program, and was authored by Michael Carney and Cynthia Shorney, Winter 1987–88.

28 "Shopping and service tasks add stress to my life": Study conducted by Eugene H. Fram and Joel Axelrod and reported in *American Demographics,* October 1990.

29 Pollster Louis Harris's research into the number of hours Americans work: "Are We All Working Too Hard?" *The Wall Street Journal,* January 4, 1990.

31 Information on companies cutting manufacturing time: "How Managers Can Succeed through Speed," *Fortune,* February 13, 1989.

31 "Citicorp Offers Mortgage Commitments in 15 Minutes": *The Wall Street Journal,* February 8, 1989, and interviews with Citicorp officials.

33 Information on the founding of Hillman/Kohan: "The Eyes Still Have It," *Inc Magazine,* November 1987, and from additional research.

34 Thanks to the research staff at the Photo Marketing Association for their help in researching the minilab revolution. Especially instructive was their 1988 publication, "Mini-Labs: Strategies for the Future," by Glenn S. Omura, Ph.D.

38 Dr. Neil Baum's quote: "How to Develop an On-Time Practice," *American Medical News,* November 24, 1989.

39 Rudyard Istvan's article, "Time-Based Competition: The New Frontier" appeared in *Management Digest,* in a special advertising supplement.

42 "We were having a helluva problem": Author interview with Fred Smith.

43 My thinking on time guarantees was greatly expanded by discussions with Dr. Eugene Fram, J. Warren McClure Research Professor at the Rochester Institute of Technology, and from his article "Ready for a Time Guarantee," *Journal of Consumer Marketing,* Fall, 1985.

43 "We are convinced that Rapid Refund has helped differentiate us": Author interview with Tom Bloch.

Driving Force 2: Convenience

51 Background information on the quick-lube industry: "In Search of Quick Bucks in Fast Lubes," *Los Angeles Times,* May 23, 1989.

52 Statistics on Southern California gas stations: "Southland Gas Stations Getting Scarcer, Bigger," *Los Angeles Times,* December 18, 1989.

52 Information on the supermarket industry: Numerous sources, including "Changing Face of Supermarkets," by Brian J. Layng, *Los Angeles Times,* March 7, 1990.

53 Success of Giant Foods: "Why Giant Foods is a Gargantuan Success," *Business Week,* December 4, 1989.

54 "In the future, telephone numbers will be associated with people, not places": "No Cords, No Wires, No Limits," *Los Angeles Times,* February 20, 1990.

54 Jan Carlzon's book is *Moments of Truth*. I quoted Carlzon from a Newstrack audio edition of the book.

62 Information on Vons supermarkets: Author interviews with Roger Stangland, chairman of Vons.

63 For information on "ease of use" see "Making the Package a Product Benefit," *Adweek,* October 3, 1988.

Driving Force 3: Age Waves

66 "The demographics have been against us": Levi Strauss chairman Peter Haas was quoted in *Fortune's 1989 Investor's Guide.*

71 Information on H.J. Heinz's Alba hot cocoa mix: "Marketers Court Older Consumers as Buying Power Shifts," *The Wall Street Journal,* April 23, 1986.

73 "Seniors buy for the experience": "The Senior Boom: How It Will Change America," *Fortune,* March 27, 1989.

73 "Simply addressing conscious wants and needs is not sufficient": "Marketing to Our Aging Population," by Charles D. Schewe, *Journal of Consumer Marketing,* Summer, 1988.

74 Background information on Club Med's changing strategy: "Club Med's 'Beautiful People' Get Older in New Ad Campaign," *Los Angeles Times,* August 17, 1989.

76 Background information on Sleep Inns: "With Labor Scarce, Service Firms Strive to Raise Productivity," *The Wall Street Journal,* June 1, 1989, and from "Labor Shortages Demand Flexibility from Service Firms," *The Service Edge* newsletter, July 1989.

79 Information on Original Research Corporation: "Taming the Labor Shortage," by Bruce G. Posner, *Inc. Magazine,* November 1989.

Driving Force 4: Choice

84 Beth Ann Krier's article "Overchoice: Have We Gone Too Far?" appeared in the *Los Angeles Times,* February 12, 1989.

85 "We hear over and over again": "Overchoice," *Los Angeles Times,* February 12, 1989.

85 Information on network television's loss of viewership: "Cable Channels, VCR Lead TV Revolution for Viewer Independence," *Los Angeles Times,* December 27, 1989.

87 For a discussion of Burger King's "have it your way" campaign, see "Guerrilla Marketing," *Inc. Magazine,* April 1987, which reviewed the book, *Marketing Warfare* by Al Ries and Jack Trout.

92 "In today's marketplace you're crazy to interpose anything between you and the consumers": Interview in *Inc. Magazine,* November 1987.

93 My discussion of the all-suite concept was informed by "Lodging Chains Sour on All-Suite Hotel," *The Wall Street Journal,* November 28, 1989.

94 "I spend my time seeing what customers see": Author interview with Debbi Fields.

Driving Force 5: Lifestyle

99 The Singer executive was John S. Rydz, who wrote about it in his book *Managing Innovation,* Ballinger Books, 1986.

103 "Our main thrust with new product development": Author interview with Stan Gault.

105 Information on the direct selling industry: "Get Ready for Shopping at Work," *Fortune,* February 15, 1988, and from "Avon's New Refrain," *Los Angeles Times,* October 26, 1989.

107 Information on Liz Claiborne, Inc.: Interviews with Jerome Chazen, chairman of Liz Claiborne, Inc., and other sources.

Driving Force 6: Discounting

130 "It's amazing that someone will actually fight traffic": "State of the Industry Report," by Jack Miller, published by his company and privately distributed.

132 Information on Help-U-Sell: Interviews with Jack Andrews, president.

133 "People are more price-conscious these days": "Casket Controversy," *Los Angeles Times,* June 24, 1989.

135 "We were the first in, kind of like McDonald's": "Discount Cruising Takes a Bruising," *Insight,* June 22, 1987.

135 For further insight into the differentiation effect, see "Little Touches Spur Wal-Mart's Rise," *The Wall Street Journal,* September 22, 1989.

138 "I always believed there was too much": Author interview with Sol Price.

140 "And nobody was really performing a service": Author interview with George Orban.

Driving Force 7: Value-Adding

146 "The consumer of the nineties will be the smartest": Interview in *Inc. Magazine,* November 1987.

150 "What allows us to be a discounter and a full-service retailer": Author interview with Richard Sharp.

154 Information on independent bookstores from "Rattling the Chains," *Time,* October 23, 1989, and other sources.

159 "You have to listen to customers": "Maverick of Dinner Houses Faces Spaghetti Shoot-Out," *The Wall Street Journal,* January 29, 1990.

Driving Force 8: Customer Service

165 Information on Nordstrom's customer service methods: "The Rise and Rise of Nordstrom," *Lear's,* October 1989, and from "Nordstrom's Push East Will Test Its Renowned Service," *The Wall Street Journal,* August 1, 1989.

166 Information on Bubbling Bath Spa & Tub Works: Interviews with Barry Fribush, and from "For You, Our Valued Customer," by Paul B. Brown, *Inc. Magazine,* January 1990.

168 Information on British Airways' customer service emphasis: "How British Airways Butters Up the Passenger," *Business Week,* March 12, 1990.

172 Information on Lexus customer service plans: "Two Days in Boot Camp—Learning to Love Lexus," *Business Week,* September 4, 1989.

172 Home Depot's service excellence was detailed in "The Fix Is In At Home Depot," *Fortune,* February 28, 1988, and interviews with company officials.

174 "To get new customers has a price": "The Art of Loving," *Inc. Magazine,* May 1989.

Driving Force 9: Techno-Edge

180 NCR background information: "Leading NCR out of the Wilderness," *Fortune,* February 18, 1980.

181 American Airlines' techno-edge discussed in "American Aims for the Sky," *Business Week,* February 20, 1989, and interviews with company officials.

185 Mrs. Fields' use of technology: "Use Technology to Manage People," *Inc. Magazine,* May 1990.

189 Professor Jack Levin's classification scheme: "Early and Late Techno Adopters," *FutureScan,* July 23, 1990.

191 Use of fax machines in innovative ways: "Fax Machines Mark New Era in Communications Revolution," *John Naisbitt's Trend Letter,* November 10, 1988.

193 Houston architect Gary Whitney's techno-edge: "The Next Step," by Tom Richman, *Inc. Magazine,* October 1989.

194 How future-focused banks are using technology to gain information power: "Banks Discover the Consumer," *Fortune,* February 12, 1990.

196 Fast-food outlets increasingly using technology: "Automation: Robots May Soon Flip Your Burger," Calvin Sims, New

York Times News Service, *Santa Barbara News Press,* August 25, 1988.

196 Warren Blanding's ideas on automating the low end and personalizing the high end: Discussed regularly in his *Customer Service Newsletter*, published in Silver Spring, MD.

Driving Force 10: Quality

201 "Our philosophy is that moviegoing should be an event": Author interview with Alan Silverman.

203 "Quality is an accurate tax return": Author interview with Tom Bloch.

210 Discussion of safety as an emerging issue, see "U.S. Auto Makers Decide Safety Sells," *The Wall Street Journal,* August 24, 1988.

213 USC professor Dana Cuff's research is discussed in "The Gap Between Use and Users of Buildings," *Los Angeles Times,* December 5, 1989.

INDEX

ABOUT THE AUTHOR

ROBERT B. TUCKER is one of America's leading authorities on unleashing innovative potential. Founder and president of The Innovation Resource, a research and executive development firm, Tucker has brought his practical, results-oriented presentations to literally thousands of individuals, trade associations and companies throughout the United States. His book, *Winning the Innovation Game,* coauthored with Denis Waitley, identified the key attributes of America's leading innovators.

To communicate with Robert Tucker, or for more information about his programs and audio/video products, contact:

The Innovation Resource
PO Box 30930
Santa Barbara, CA 93130

(805) 682-1012